# From Man to Man

*by Henry Ritter, Jr., M.D.*

*with Owen Spann*

# FROM MAN TO MAN

Published in San Francisco by

HARPER & ROW, PUBLISHERS

New York, Hagerstown, San Francisco, London

FIRST EDITION

Designed by Leigh McLellan

Library of Congress Cataloging in Publication Data

Ritter, Henry.
   From man to man.

   Bibliography: p. 151
   Includes index.
   1. Sex instruction for men. I. Spann, Owen,
joint author. II. Title.
HQ36.R54 1979 613.9′52    78-20591
ISBN 0-06-250700-1

79 80 81 82 83 10 9 8 7 6 5 4 3 2 1

# Dedication

We wish to thank all women everywhere, and especially our wives, Mary Ritter and Nancie Spann

# Contents

# *Acknowledgments*

WE HAVE NOT attempted to write another "how-to" book, nor dispense specific medical advice. That should come from your own doctor. Thirty-three years of active medical practice and twenty-five years of active radio interviewing, between us, serve as the basis for this book. Along the creative way, we are indebted to the cogent listeners of KGO Radio, San Francisco, who shared their questions and concerns with us. We wish to give special thanks for the help given us by Jim Keating and Chet Casselman, KOVR-TV, as well as Cliff Wells, David Goodstein, our editor Bill Alexander, who has been an excellent sounding board, and Linda Purrington, our copy editor who did so much more.

# *Foreword*

BY OWEN SPANN

I AM IN the "talk" business. Throughout twenty years in radio and television, I have probably interviewed some 25,000 people, representing every walk of life. I have chatted with a bevy of celebrities ranging from Jimmy Carter to Julia Child to "Joey," a reported Mafia "hit man." Every imaginable subject has been covered: food, clothing, shelter, current events, politics, sports, and, most certainly, sex.

In the early 1970s, I began to notice an absolute deluge of sexual books written with the female in mind. First came the early wave of feminist books, asking Mrs. Housewife if she were truly happy in her split-level suburban life? Next came the gynecologists and psychologists, discussing various methods of birth control and how to overcome frigidity. And, finally, a series of books put it all together for today's sexually liberated woman. The result has been women who can candidly talk about their various partners, discuss masturbation, and automatically assume the "male superior" position in bed.

At this point, I began to wonder if my program were becoming too slanted toward our female listeners. What about the *male* viewpoint? How is today's man handling his sexually free mate? If a gynecologist could best answer feminine problems, where do I turn for information on the male animal? To a urologist, of course. Having known Dr. Henry

Ritter for many years, I first invited him on my program in November 1976.

The immediate reaction to that first show was astonishing. Since people are able to remain anonymous when calling a talk station, they feel free to express their innermost thoughts almost immediately. And anonymity is the secret that allows men and women to ask questions that badly need to be answered, questions that they had been unable to ask their own physicians face-to-face.

That first program brought forth an avalanche of comments, many of which centered around the fascination that both sexes seem to have with the penis and what its proper size should be. One man was concerned, not about the length of his penis, but about the fact that every time he had an erection, his organ became crooked—and bent at an angle. Another man claimed he had devised the perfect system of birth control. He had taught himself how to ejaculate backward, into the bladder, instead of out through the penis. A mother called in to express concern that her baby boy had been born with only one testicle descended. Finally, there was a tragic call from a man who had been brutally sexually assaulted while in jail for a minor traffic violation.

I was most impressed with the way Dr. Ritter answered these people: with humor, with sympathy, with concern, and, in one case, with a dire warning that a woman should get her husband under a doctor's care immediately.

I invited Dr. Ritter back again and again. Our callers seem to be equally divided between men and women. It has become a regular monthly event on KGO Radio. One day, after we had done two year's worth of shows, I remarked to Henry that we should put all this information into a book that would be very beneficial to most couples today.

I said, "Isn't it a shame we don't have tapes of all the shows we have done together?"

I'll never forget his casual answer: "I have every word of every program taped and transcribed. It's a *must* for reference and medical back-up."

So the book was born. Actual questions from real people make up its base. Along the way, we have filled in the missing gaps to present the full story of modern man and the way he functions (or *should* function).

You may laugh at some of the questions and cry at others. You may think "How lucky *I* am," or you may head for your nearest medical center, if some of the warning signs apply to you. But I guarantee you will learn about your own body. And so will your mate.

# *Foreword*    BY HENRY RITTER, JR., M.D.

LIFE TODAY IS a series of traffic signs: STOP. GO. YIELD. MERGE. ONE-WAY. DO NOT ENTER. Even SEX has become computerized. We are being told how, when, where, and how many times to have sex. And we must follow these directions in proper sequence. In order to arrive at sexual ecstasy, (6) we must proceed through steps 1, 2, 3, 4, 5 as prescribed.

While *men* are trying to figure this whole thing out mathematically, *women* of today are enjoying unprecedented freedom. Think of the deluge of magazine articles informing the liberated female that not only can the *perfect orgasm* be hers but also that the perfect orgasm is her God-given *right*.

Is her mate up to it, or he is more apt to hide in a corner, questioning his own sexual prowess and wondering what happened to his potency? Certainly it is time to consider what effect today's changing sexual roles have had on the male animal. But to do that we must examine just what the male animal is really made of—hardly "snips and snails and puppy-dog tails." Substitute, instead, terms like *penis, testes, bladder,* and *prostate,* and you begin to have a better idea.

To learn where man is today, let's start where *he* started, at birth. Should he be circumcised, or is that a deadly, traumatic experience?

Then, what are his levels of development through puberty? His first sexual experience may very well be with one of today's liberated young women. If *she* is the one who suggests "going to bed," what might his reactions be?

How does today's young man get his sex education: from his peer group, from TV, in school, at home? In spite of all the brouhaha about our modern teenagers, I personally feel *they* don't know any more than *we* did about sex, which was next to nothing. I also look on sex education in the public schools as an unmitigated disaster.

How do problems of *impotence* get started in the first place? And they *will* because, every man, at some time, will experience periods where he is unable to have an erection.

In examining the male animal, it will be necessary to deal with some myths from the streets: that masturbation will drive you crazy; that ginseng root and oysters are aphrodisiacs; and that the length of your penis determines your ability as a lover.

What part do drugs play in achieving sexual fantasies? While cocaine and marijuana may seem an immediate turn-on, few people realize that their continued use could result in a *decrease* of the male hormones, an *increase* in female hormones, and an eventual tendency for the man to grow breasts.

While many heterosexuals snicker quietly about "fags" and "queers," how much really *is* known about the homosexual? How does he make love? What special physical problems does he have?

Is venereal disease on the rise or decline? One thing for sure: VD has changed from centuries-old syphilis and gonorrhea to supergonorrhea and Herpes II, a new virus you may never get rid of.

What's *new* in contraceptives? What's new is *old*. We are seeing a rush back to the basics—condoms and diaphragms. Today's women are turning away from the chemistry of the pill and the irritation of the I.U.D., deciding that the side effects may outweigh the benefits.

The ultimate in contraception, of course, is sterilization. Since a vasectomy is easier on the male than a tubal ligation is on his mate, we'll analyze this procedure from all aspects. What is the operation, and how much does it cost? Will there be much pain? When will you be "safe"? And, most importantly, are you emotionally ready to undergo this procedure?

Since almost 20 percent of the married couples today are barren, what about those who want children but have been unable to have them? How can they be helped, short of a trip to the test tubes? There are many things an infertile man can try first that are much less complicated.

Let's explore the male animal together: from his morning erection to his hernia, from his love life to his urinary problems in the middle of the night, from infancy to old age.

Sure, every man is going to have problems. But if he hopes for a *continuing healthy sex life,* he must have a *continuing healthy sex life.* If that sounds like double-talk to you, let me explain.

Throughout his lifetime, our man will probably go through temporary times when he "can't get it up," when he "comes" too quickly, and when he cannot communicate with his mate, who may be turned off by sex. The more he *avoids* or *ignores* these issues, the more he turns away, fearing inadequacy or rejection, the *worse* each of these situations can get.

If there is one underlying philosophy I would like to stress, it is this: USE IT OR LOSE IT.

If man is to cope with today's changing society, it's time for him to stop worrying so much and inventing problems where none exist. It is time for him to learn more about his own body, and to share this knowledge with his sexual partner. With her help, many of his problems can be easily eliminated, leading to a new growth experience for *both* of them.

The title of this book is *From Man to Man.* Yet, if you do find your lady love sneaking a peak at a chapter on premature ejaculation, for example, don't be angry. Congratulate her. Equal rights pertain to sex, too. And it takes two to attain a fulfilling relationship. Just don't be surprised if you hear remarks like: *"I didn't know that!!"*

# Part One

# *In the Beginning*

BEFORE WE EXAMINE twentieth-century American man, his successes and his hang-ups, let's find out how he got where he is today. What's involved in raising a male child, and what should you look out for along the way?

From birth to puberty, a boy will go through various phases: oral, anal, phallic, oedipal, and genital. The majority of boy babies are born with the usual biological equipment. In other words, they've got the correct number of organs and will, in time, develop sexually.

We are sexual beings from the moment of birth. An infant will start with that sucking reflex that you see in all nursing babies, be they breast or bottle fed. This is one of the basic sexual stimuli that will last throughout his lifetime. We see older children sucking their thumbs and we see adults smoking, seeking to gratify their original oral need.

From the time of birth, the boy child may have an erection. He may even be seen to masturbate, not by reaching for his penis, but by rocking back and forth on his belly in the crib, stimulating his penis against his diapers or bedclothes. And that little fellow has the same reaction an adult would have. He breathes a little heavier and faster, his face becomes flushed, and his heart rate goes up. This whole procedure is quite typical of an orgasm, except, of course, his sexual apparatus isn't producing fluid yet. Girl babies are just as sensitive in the genital area. The anal stage starts when the baby begins to control his bowels and his urine, usually at about the two-year-old level. Here, he is involved in whether or not to eliminate or control his stool and urine. If he retains it, it gives him a sense of warmth. If he excretes it, it offers him a sense of pleasure. Unfortunately, many bad sex practices are instilled in the child at this stage. For example, the parent, while bathing the baby, may clean the genital area last, thereby implying that this part is "dirty." It is amazing how young in life the baby can pick up these bad vibes from a parent.

I often see older children with urinary problems that may have originated during this anal stage. To add to the difficulties, I don't always know what *terms* the family has used for the various body functions. Do they refer to urinating as "tinkle," "ta ta," or "tee-tee"? Parents certainly don't have to resort to street vulgarisms, but a penis is a *penis*, and a vagina is a *vagina*. Urination is *urination* or *wetting*. Defecation is *stool* or *potty*.

I must admit I get a bit confused when a mother talks about numbers "1, 2, 3, 4, and 5." What on earth are "3, 4, and 5"? Such euphemisms carry forward in the child's life and can make him sexually immature. In his teens, he may still be talking about "tee-tee" and end up the laughingstock of his peers. The more parents shy away from calling a spade a spade, or a penis a penis, the more they reinforce the idea that the sex organs are bad or dirty.

The phallic stage (three to four years old) is a time of experimentation. The boy learns that he has a penis but that a girl hasn't. The little girl may go through a period of penis envy; while the little boy may fear the loss of his. The boy may fondle his penis, not in any sexual connotation, but purely because it feels good and to make sure his penis is still there.

In the oedipal stage, about age five, the boy sexually and psychologically aligns himself against the parent of his own sex. In other words, he is competing with his father for the affection of his mother, or other female members of the family. Fortunately for all concerned, this is a short-lived period.

In the genital stage, he absolutely delights in urinating or having a good bowel movement. Don't we all? Expelling wastes becomes a pleasure. But he may also take great delight in retaining his fluid or stool. He has the stimulus to "go," but he holds back, which gives him a kind of genital stimulation.

An overlapping period of latency then takes over until prepuberty. Most often, the boy will want to team up with other boys. Girls aren't exactly "yukky" to him, but they will only be asked to join an activity on a random basis. The male peer group looms supreme. Your son may start bringing home dirty words from school. He may test your attitudes against those of his friends' parents. Toward the end of the latent years, as he approaches prepuberty, you'll start to find games like "Spin the Bottle" being played at mixed gatherings. Yes, they still *do* play "Spin the Bottle."

The prepuberty stage usually begins from about the age of 10 to 12 years. This is right before the boy gets that big big male hormonal shot of testosterone, which deepens his voice, causes the major growth spurt, and has him looking in the mirror at what might be the beginning of a whisker. He starts to learn about masturbating and has probably already had his first "wet dream". That first wet dream is usually an accidental occurence, where there is an involuntary ejaculation of fluid from his prostate while he is asleep. It is often accompanied by erotic dreams.

As he moves into puberty itself, he is most aware that something is happening to him. He may join with other boys in group exploratory activities, such as mutual masturbating and contests to see who can ejaculate the farthest. His peer group may compare notes on who "scored" last night, or, at least, who claimed to have scored.

The hormonal tide now is really high. At this point, it is difficult to separate puberty from adolescence. One may be more physical, the other more emotional, but it all is happening at the same time. In the years from thirteen to fifteen, he becomes somewhat gawky, with over-extending arms and legs. As he nears eighteen, he starts to accumulate body fat and begins to fill out. As he nears the new age of adulthood, his parents are preparing him to cut the cord and to get ready for that world out there, but, emotionally, he is still a boy.

Is he ready for manhood? During the puberty years, he has gone through periods both of dependence on his family and of desire to be independent of it. As his male hormone supply has built up, he may have become sloppy, crude, defiant, and unruly. His body hair has been appearing more fully. His penis and scrotum have been enlarging, and his voice has been lowering. He may have been worrying about the *size* of his penis and his sudden upsurge in sexual feelings. All these factors take him by surprise, even if he has read about them and discussed them with his peer group.

And society doesn't help. At the turn of the century, the human life span was twenty years shorter than it is today. Therefore, a youngster had to reproduce at an earlier age in order to maintain the family unit. Now, however, although we are living longer, procreative pressure on the young man should have lessened. Actually, it has increased, because of the world around us.

He is inundated by the sensual images of television advertising. To further confuse him, his parents' attitude is often contradictory. They may say, "Be grown up. Why aren't you dating?" Yet at the same time they may be demanding obedience, dependence, and sexual abstinence from their children.

Parents who view their boy's teenage years as "monster years" might stop for a moment to realize that these may be "monster years" for him, too.

*Q. My little boy's penis is so small—is there a good chance he will always be underdeveloped?*

No, no, no, no, no!! I've heard this question so many times from mothers, I should tape-record my answer.

As your son reaches prepuberty, his penis will grow right along with the rest of him, both in length and circumference.

But I have never seen a truly underdeveloped penis in all my years of practice. Call it what you will—a micropenis, a penette—I have never seen it. There is a rare occurrence where the penis never grows from its infantile birth state. But if that had been the case here, the mother should have already known about the problem from being married to the boy's father, since it is often hereditary.

Occasionally, I am shocked when a mother will bring in a six or seven-year-old when there really *is* something wrong with the penis, or with a testicle that hasn't descended. I can't believe that she hadn't noticed it until that late in his life.

Again, size is not the major factor. If later in his life he can get it up, get it in, and deliver the semen, he's fine, and so is his mate.

*Q. I think all mothers are concerned about how their sons are endowed. I have two boys. With my firstborn, I could barely even find his penis. My next son was born looking like King Kong? Can you explain this?*

Can YOU? Whether you know it or not, you had a lot to do with it.

Until the sixth week of pregnancy, there is no sex differentiation in the developing fetus. From then on, the mother's hormones influence the growth and sexual development of your child. You may have had a different hormonal flow with each pregnancy, thereby influencing your babies' genitals. Another factor may have been the cell development within the fetus.

I'm sure you've noticed by now that your sons have pretty much equaled out. As the old show biz adage says, "Even if you have a poor dress rehearsal, don't worry—you'll have a great opening night."

*Q. Why is it that, if you compare a group of twelve-year-old boys and girls, the girls seem to be taller? Then, if you compare them again at seventeen or so, the boys have caught up and shot ahead.*

Growth and puberty go hand in hand. While boys reach puberty anywhere from twelve to fourteen years of age, the time of menarche has been advancing steadily for girls. Since the turn of this century, girls are now starting to menstruate eight months earlier. It is not unusual for a young girl to begin her periods by the age of eleven, or younger. Don't ask me why, but it has been moving up a month per decade. So, with an earlier puberty start, she also starts her growth period sooner.

As far as *sexuality* goes, the boy advances faster. Once he is into his puberty period, he really bursts ahead. The problem is that he peaks out sexually around the age of twenty-two, whereas the young woman builds slowly to a peak in her middle or late twenties. An ideal sexual match would pair a twenty-year-old man with a woman ten years his senior. Of course, sex is not an Olympic event, but such a pair would reach the apex of physical matchability.

*Q. At what age can young children conceive a baby?*

In today's society, it would be possible for two eleven-year-olds to add to the growing population. Usually, the boy would have to be almost thirteen. The girl, however, can become pregnant any time after her first few menstrual periods.

*Q. You mentioned that, before ever having masturbated, a child may experience a "wet dream." What is it, actually, and how does it occur?*

If you don't know what it is, you've certainly missed one of life's most unexpected surprises.

A wet dream, or nocturnal emission in politer terms, is a sexual turn-on that occurs during sleep. There is a period of stimulation, either through fantasy or the friction of bedclothes, that creates an erection and eventually an ejaculation. Wet dreams most commonly occur between the age of twelve and twenty, and will happen to nine out of ten boys. In older men, a wet dream can also be brought on by an irritation within the prostate gland. Or it can result from a full bladder or full rectum stimulating the area. Incidentally, the same thing can happen to a woman, perhaps through wadding up of the bedclothes between her legs.

Back to the young boy for a moment. This accidental but normal occurrence is usually associated with great shame. The youngster may be afraid to tell his mother. He may get up and change his pajamas and bed sheets in the middle of the night, hoping no one will notice what has happened.

*Q. Once a mother has noticed this sort of accident, is this the time to sit down and have the famous "birds and bees" chat, or should she ignore it?*

Since we're talking about a ten to twelve-year-old, if you haven't already discussed sex with him, you *bet* this is the time to do it. And I mean the very next day.

Unfortunately, the heart-to-heart talks that fathers are supposed to have with their sons rarely take place. And father to daughter? *Almost never.* Most fathers are too embarrassed to discuss this sort of thing with their female offspring, since by then most of the daughters are already becoming attractive young women.

Getting back to our parent-and-son chat, by the time you sit your son down, you're going to be amazed at how much he already knows. In some areas, he may know more than you do. But remember, he will only absorb what he is ready to absorb. Somehow, kids let us know how much they want to learn at various stages of their lives: "I'm ready to hear about A and B, but I'm not ready for C and D." As a parent, you'll find his interest diminishing if you go beyond what he actually wants to know.

I personally feel that you will not make your child promiscuous by discussing sexuality with him. I also believe that, if you have been open in your discussions and have been loving and affectionate, the child will equate sexuality with a warm, protective home. If the youngster is being raised in a single-parent household, with a constant array of new faces at the breakfast table, you're in for trouble. He is learning promiscuity at an early age, and, as he grows older, he may find himself pressured into relationships before he is ready. In the more intelligent single-parent households, the lover is brought in after the child goes to bed and leaves before breakfast.

*Q. I know this sounds stupid, but for those of us who simply can't talk it out—I mean the "facts of life"—are there any books that you can recommend—material we can go over together with our children?*

I wish I could be more helpful, but there isn't much up-to-date material available for the older generation. One of the main reasons for this sad state of affairs is that there just doesn't seem to be much demand. In talking with my pediatric colleagues, I was informed that parents simply aren't requesting this sort of information. Parents are already reluctant to get into this area, assuming unwisely that the schools have taken over this function completely.

Also, the child and his pediatrician aren't close anymore. He may see his doctor once or twice a year for a checkup, usually when he's well. This is probably because of good nutrition and better medical care, but that child-doctor closeness is gone. We are a very mobile society. Families move frequently; it is the rare child who grows up with one pediatrician.

It seems that many parents find it hard to discuss the sexual facts of life without either stumbling all over themselves, being embarrassed, or getting outrageously uncomfortable and red in the face. The best current literature that I have personally reviewed includes "What to Tell Your Child About Sex" (Child Study Press, 1974), "Where Did I Come From?" (Mayle, 1976), "What's Happening to Me?" (Mayle, 1975), and "Show Me" (McBride and Hardt, 1975).

*Q. You mentioned that "you'd be amazed at how much your child already knows." Might this be misinformation he picked up from his peers?*

Not necessarily. In *Better Sex, Better Marriage* (1978), Dr. Robert Kaufmann, who is a minister, psychologist, and marriage counselor, recalled the time his ten-year-old son picked up an article on "The Psychosomatic Aspects of Frigidity."

The following conversation then took place:

*Father:* "What paper do you have?"

*Son:* "The Psycho-so-matic Aspects of Fridguh-ditty."

*Father:* "You can read it if you know what it's about."

*Son* (without hesitation): "It's about someone who doesn't like fucking."

*Father:* "Read it."

*Q. When do children really get into masturbation?*

It appears that both sexes become serious about this in their early teens. Boys seem to learn from one another and are much more communicative about it within their peer groups. Girls learn to masturbate primarily through accidental discovery and do not discuss their own sexual behavior as openly as boys do.

To give you the exact statistics on the male animal, only a negligible percentage of boys masturbate to orgasm by the age of ten. From then on, the incidence rate climbs dramatically. By the age of thirteen, about 65 percent of the boys have masturbated. And, as a young man approaches twenty, if he is *ever* going to do it, he probably has already.

*Q. If I find my son masturbating, should I stop him? Isn't it injurious to his health?*

I would agree there is a time and place for everything; and I would hardly condone a child's masturbating at the check-out stand in my supermarket. But is it injurious? Absolutely not.

Why does a boy masturbate? He may be fantasizing as to what his future sex life may be like, or he may be defying you as a parent. He may be trying to upset you, to test your authority. You might consider masturbation to be improper, not quite respectable. And so you punish your son, thus implying that harm will come to him if he continues doing this.

There is no end to the *supposed* results of masturbation: insanity, epilepsy, headaches, deafness, and hallucinations. Perhaps you were once told that your face would break out in pimples or that warts would form on the hand you used? There is absolutely no evidence to support any of these "dangers," no deleterious effects. In fact, it can help to relieve teen-age tension.

As your teenager moves into adulthood, masturbation will be abandoned for the more mature and fulfilling outlet of coitus.

*Q. How do you feel about nudity? Our family has never made any "big deal" about wearing clothes around the house. But now our ten-year-old son seems to be getting uncomfortable with the situation.*

As a boy grows up, the chances are he has seen his parents nude. That is perfectly normal. In fact, he has probably been bathed with one of his siblings on many occasions. This may be the best way for him to learn about nudity and to satisfy his natural curiosity. By being natural, the youngster develops a wholesome, natural feeling about his body. If he grows up in an uninhibited atmosphere, he will probably have fewer sexual hang-ups. So, if he is accustomed to family nudity, he is less likely to view nudity as shocking or repulsive or overstimulating.

As he grows older, he has already been inundated by nudity in the media. Many a "PG" (parental guidance recommended) movie today has at least one nude scene. Nudity on the screen and nudity at home become two different things. He may be confused. What is perfectly OK in the home is forbidden in the outside world. Even professionals in this field can't agree on whether family nudity is good or bad. Your son is already in the sexually curious years. Once he reaches the prepuberty age, he may be getting sexually excited. Perhaps you should reevaluate your family's lifestyle for the next few years as he is growing up.

*Q. My fourteen-year-old son loves sports but thinks up any excuse to cut his physical education class. Why?*

I can think of two reasons right away.

First, he may dread the locker room, which involves undressing and taking showers with the other guys. His classmates may have already developed pubic hair and bigger genitals, whereas he may still be in the "Cub Scout" category.

Secondly, the way school teams are put together may be a factor. Maybe he is getting the hell knocked out of him. School squads are usually selected by age, not by physiological groupings. One fourteen-year-old may be built like a pro linebacker while another may not. Your son, who may weigh 90 pounds, could find himself pitted against a 130-pounder in his same age group. By cutting physical education classes, he may be doing his best to prevent personal mayhem.

## Circumcision

Is this statement true or false: "The act of circumcision began as a Jewish tradition to promote better hygiene"?

If you answered "true," go to the back of the class. This may come as a surprise, but, it all began with the ancient Egyptians, possibly 6,000 years ago. And hygiene was the farthest thing from their minds. The foreskin was a trophy of war.

Originally, the Egyptians who were victorious in battle came back with the heads of the warriors they had defeated, to show how many men they had killed. At this point, history blurs a bit, but perhaps the heads became a bit cumbersome to carry back to Cairo. So the head gave way to the genital organs as the spoils of war, and eventually the foreskin became the trophy of triumph.

Then, around the fourth century BC, the priests of Egypt began having themselves circumcised, feeling it would keep their bodies cleaner. Circumcision became the mark of the priesthood. Soon the nobility picked up the custom, both as an aid to hygiene and as a symbol of importance. In fact, just as we hold our right hand aloft with our left hand resting on a Bible while taking an oath, the ancient Egyptian raised his circumcised phallis in token of sincerity.

The early Israelites, Semitic relatives of the Egyptians, accepted the belief that the foreskin was, from time of birth, a source of annoyance, danger, suffering, and possible death. So they took up the rite themselves. According to the book of Genesis, Abraham was the first man to perform circumcision—on himself, his son, and his servant. And Abraham was ninety-nine years old at the time.

There was one major difference in the two traditions. In Judaism, the circumcision, or "bris," was performed on a new-born baby on his eighth day of life. The Egyptians waited until the boy was thirteen years of age (Paige, 1978).

In modern America, by the end of the 1930s, about three-fourths of all middle-class families were having their sons circumcised, as more and more women began to enter hospitals to give birth. Today, approximately 87 percent of all male babies are being circumcised in the United States.

The only other country in the world that reports almost as high a frequency is Australia. Aborigines there were into circumcision as far back as 10,000 years ago.

Do not be swayed by the fact that Abraham and the Egyptian priests practiced "do-it-yourself" circumcision. Do-it-yourself is not for you.

*Q. I have heard that if you circumcise a baby, he will lose a part of his penis. Is this true?*

Let me explain what circumcision is and then you be the judge.

The penis is composed of a shaft that extends from base of the scrotum out to the mushroom-capped tip, which is called the *glans*. A very thin fold of skin extends from the shaft over this tip.

In circumcision, only this extra fold is removed, leaving the shaft intact and exposing the tip. It is very much like peeling the skin from a banana. The size of the organ is unchanged.

*Q. Do rabbis still perform this operation?*

Let me correct an old myth right now. Circumcision really never was the function of the rabbi. A man called a *mohel* actually has that responsibility. He uses a razor-sharp, forked blade and is quite skillful at trimming off the foreskin. With an unpracticed man this can cause problems, but the *mohel* usually is a very accomplished practitioner.

*Q. How common is this religious type of circumcision today?*

Not common at all, because of the small number of orthodox Jews left in America. And there are very few *mohels* practicing today.

Recently, I did take part in an unique circumcision when a forty-five-year-old man converted to Judaism on the occasion of his marriage. To make everything kosher, the circumcision required both the hospital surgical staff and a fully capped-and-gowned rabbi. Intermingled with the hospital's public address system and the noise of the anesthesia machine were the singing prayers of the rabbi. A novel experience, to say the least.

*Q. When should the baby be circumcised?*

A day or so after the birth. Certainly before the mother and baby leave the hospital, all things being normal.

*Q. How would circumcision fit in with the theories of Dr. Frederick LeBoyer, who believes in a nonviolent birth with soft lights, quiet music, and warm water?*

If you totally accept the LeBoyer theory, then you would not have your baby circumcised at all. I think the LeBoyer method is fine for the birth process itself, but as far as I'm concerned, *every* male child should be circumcised. One exception would be if the baby has a deformity of his penis. For example, sometimes, the urinary opening occurs further down the shaft or on the front of the scrotal area. This is called a *hypospadias* and would not warrant circumcision. Or, perhaps, the baby was delivered at home, where circumcision could not be done. Premature birth can also be a factor in delaying circumcision in the new born.

*Q. What are your feelings on the necessity of submitting a newborn boy to the trauma of circumcision?*

I don't consider it to be traumatic. The problems do not begin at birth.

I have seen too many complications arise in later years with youngsters who were *not* circumcised.

As life goes on, men who are sexually active may have many female partners. Many of these men will never practice proper genital hygiene. Because of the foreskin, it is more difficult to clean themselves adequately after intercourse. Consequently they frequently develop an inflammation from material coated on the tip of the penis and trapped beneath the foreskin. The foreskin then tends to scar over the tip of the penis, causing constant soreness and painful erection.

All of this will eventually lead them to adult circumcision, which is a more complicated procedure than on the newborn. Interestingly enough, I have performed more adult circumcisions in the last few years than in all the previous years of my practice.

*Q. I didn't have my baby circumcised when he was born eight months ago. If I have it done now, I am concerned about the pain and the use of an anesthetic.*

We are using a very interesting anesthetic in pediatrics for circumcision in young children. It is a substance called Ketamine, which is given by injection, not inhalation. Ketamine does not put the child to sleep. He experiences absolutely no pain and afterwards can't remember a thing.

I would keep the child in the hospital for the day of his circumcision so that I could watch him to be sure there is no excessive bleeding and that he urinates easily.

*Q. What if something goes wrong and you get a botched-up operation?*

Complications seldom happen. The three most serious—infection, hemorrhaging, trauma—occur in only 1 percent of all circumcisions. The other 99 percent of the time all goes well.

*Q. My little boy was circumcised at birth. Now, he is five, and the tissue around the penis seems to have grown over it. There are little scars that connect the penis tip to the edge of the foreskin. My doctor suggests waiting a few years to correct this, so it won't affect him physically as well as psychologically.*

I disagree. I think the correction should be done immediately, if not yesterday.

Your son is already aware of the problem in his genital area. From your description, the cut edge of the foreskin should have been separated from the tip of the penis after his circumcision. It would be too painful to separate this scar tissue as an office procedure. It should be done in a hospital.

Don't wait! Have this taken care of right now.

*Q. My boyfriend has trouble with his foreskin. He can't pull it back all the way to clean himself. When he has an erection, it is very painful because the skin doesn't retract. I read that it is possible to have an incision made in his foreskin to take care of this, without going through a complete circumcision.*

This condition is known as *phimosis.* Yes, there is an operative procedure available called a *dorsal slit.* A single cut is made at the top of the penis, through the foreskin, which permits it to retract. However, this leaves a hanging wattle of skin, very similar to the underneck of a turkey. It's rather unpleasant because that extra piece of foreskin can easily get caught in a zipper. I'm sure all men have had this experience at one time or another. Since this could happen regularly I favor a full circumcision rather than a dorsal slit.

*Q. Is it a painful operation for an adult?*

Not at all. It is usually done with a local anesthetic. Applying ice and compression to the operative site will take care of most of the discomfort afterwards.

*Q. How long is the recovery time before it heals?*

You can urinate immediately, but since an erection will be painful, lovemaking should wait approximately one week.

This really isn't much of a problem because, for the first few days, an erection is the *last* thing you'd want.

*Q. My husband has never been circumcised, and he is twenty-five years old. If he has this done, could he get a vasectomy at the same time?*

Yes. The two procedures could be done together, either in the hospital or in a doctor's office. I personally don't like to do office circumcisions. Surgically clean conditions are easier to maintain in a hospital setting, and there is less chance of complications.

Remember, if he does want *both* operations at the same time, he should plan well in advance. With regard to vasectomies, new federal and state regulations require a seventy-two-hour wait between the time that he gives his written consent for sterilization and the time that the operation is performed. Recuperation time for both procedures is approximately three days. Painless sexual activity can be resumed in a week.

*Q. Is it true that once you are circumcised sex is never quite as good as before?*

From a personal standpoint, I wouldn't know, since I'm circumcised. In everything I've read, and from personal consultations with my own patients, however, there is no difference.

*Q. To answer your last question, I have had it both ways. I was circum-cised at age thirty-five, and there is no difference in my enjoyment. I felt that if I wanted a clean woman, it was only fair that I be clean, too.*

You are to be congratulated on the importance you attach to genital cleanliness, which is one of the reasons I feel so strongly about circumcision. One man told me that having the foreskin there is like making love with a pair of boots on. I frequently hear from other men that they enjoy the sex act *more* after circumcision.

We live in a mobile society. People rarely live out their lives in the community in which they are born and often find themselves in areas where genital hygiene is impossible to maintain.

In the uncircumcised male, beneath that extra length of skin that covers the tip of the penis, a cheesy substance forms, called *smegma*. It's very difficult *not* to have smegma form, because one skin surface is secreting against the other and because additional material is introduced into the area at the time of sexual contact.

This smegma is a breeding ground for bacteria and viruses, leading to genital infectious herpes or cancer of the penis. We are seeing a higher incidence of cancer of the cervix in the female sexual partners of these uncircumcised men.

# The Birds and the Bees and Sex Education

I recoil in horror when I hear people boast about today's teenagers as being the "with it generation," totally sexually aware and free of their parents' hang-ups. After more than a decade of intensive sex education in our schools, let's look at the facts.

FACT (Department of Health, Education, and Welfare): "A million American teenage girls become pregnant each year. This will account for one out of five births in the United States, as 600,000 of these girls decline the abortion route and carry their babies to term. The cost to the American taxpayer is $2,200 for the first year alone, per baby, for those in the lower economic brackets."

FACT (Family Planning Perspectives): *"Three times* more American girls became pregnant in 1976 than in 1971."

FACT *(American Journal of Obstetrics and Gynecology):* "We are no longer just talking about the lower-income and minority groups. We are in the midst of a teenage pregnancy *explosion,* particularly among the middle-class whites."

FACT: The National Center for Health Statistics: "Four out of ten American teens are now engaging in premarital sex."

Does this sound as if sex education has worked?

Writing in *Science News,* Joan Arehart-Treichel interviewed a group of today's teenage girls and was astounded at what she heard:

1. "I thought you had to be seventeen to become pregnant."
2. After having an abortion, a fifteen-year-old was told she would receive lunch. She asked, with pathetic naivete, "Do I need to bring lunch money?"
3. Another teenager: "Sex is fun. Birth control is messy or dangerous. Abortions are wrong, and babies are cute. So what's the big deal?"

Now, in no way can I lay the responsibility of today's baby binge on school sex education programs alone. Let's look at other factors: television, parents, and peer pressure.

*Newsweek,* February 28, 1978: "Sex is replacing violence on television. Sexual pressures from society, in turn, are igniting the already explosive sexual drives of adolescents and further eroding their generally poor ability to delay gratification of any kind."

Television, indeed, *is* helping to teach our children that all their physical desires can be satisfied right now. But television is not reality. If an actor gets shot on TV, and an hour later shows up on another drama, is that reality? If "Charlie" instructs one of his "Angels" to infiltrate a mob and win at any cost, is that reality?

Television, like the movies of old, glorifies the "haves": the ones who have pretty clothes, custom-made suits, and sports cars. Can you blame a youngster for watching all this pap and wondering why *he* or *she* doesn't have all these goodies?

In the summer of 1978, NBC-TV ran a special on Marin County, California, one of the nation's most affluent areas. The program depicted a group of overprivileged adults being massaged with peacock feathers and luxuriating in hot tubs in a rather pathetic search for "happiness." The title of that show summed it all up: "I Want It All Now." Even though NBC has since been censured for staging some of the events, this underlying philosophy persists among many people today.

Like parent, like child. They want it all now. Including sex.

Again, Joan Arehart-Treichel: "Many parents today do not argue for abstinence among their children, but rather encourage them to use birth control; or they simply ignore the subject of sex altogether."

Pauline Seitz, a nurse-midwife, reported, "The kids hold that birth control takes away the spontaneity of sex or pollutes the body," meaning the side effects of oral contraceptives and I.U.D.'s.

In California in 1977, more than one in nine young women, between the ages of fifteen and nineteen, became pregnant. Incredible as it may seem, many teenagers look upon sex as a transition from childhood to adulthood, relying on pregnancy to automatically make them "grown up." With more and more of these unmarried girls opting to keep their babies, the school dropout rate is up, as are child abuse cases and welfare payments.

Have you had enough already? Are today's teenagers truly sexually aware?

Hardly. Apparently, they are no better off than their counterparts of a generation or two ago, except for one aspect. They are more willing to live dangerously, to try it once. And if they don't like it, they keep trying until they do.

*Q. I thought this book was called* From Man to Man. *Why are you delving so deeply into the subject of teenage girls?*

Who gets a girl pregnant? It isn't a bird or a bee. Who helps her pass syphillis, gonorrhea, and herpes back and forth? It's not a flower.

This may be our one truly liberated chapter, because liberation has brought forth assertiveness on the part of many women. Think back a generation when often a young man would come up with a line like, "I wish I could get into her pants." Now we are seeing an opposite situation where many a girl is trying to figure a way to have the boy get into *her* pants.

The beginning of puberty is like sap flowing up a tree in the spring. I hate to keep harping on those early teenage pregnancy statistics, but all these girls certainly are not being raped.

You only have to sit in on a teen rap session to see how verbally open the girls have become. Much of this "liberation" is only verbal, but I feel they have not only caught up, but also they have surpassed the boys of twenty years ago. Girls, too, want to experience love and closeness from individuals other than their parents. The pill has given them that freedom. But the pill has brought along side effects, other than the usual body chemistry problems.

The pill does not guarantee them a satisfying sexual experience, nor does it necessarily provide a lasting relationship. And the pill does not protect them from sexually transmitted diseases, now rising at an epidemic rate.

*Q. If a girl propositions a boy, can't he just say no?*

Sure he can. But then he's got to worry about what *she* is going to say to the gang. Since she has been rebuffed, will the word spread that he is gay or too closely attached to Mommy?

If he agrees and hops in the sack with her, will she tell her friends that he was "quick like a bunny" and a lousy lover? And, who *isn't*, the first few times out of the paddock?

The young man is in a no-win situation, both physically and emotionally. He may badly need some adult to talk to, either his father or family doctor, and may be too scared to open his mouth.

*Q. How do you feel about the sex education classes being taught in our schools?*

Badly. Much of the information that is being disseminated now is quite impersonal. I don't feel that many of these courses are getting down to detail. I have sat in on some of these sessions and talked with the students afterward. It's been quite a shock to me that the students feel that the teacher was fine, as far as a blackboard blueprint was concerned, but that the nuts and bolts of the sexual act were missing.

My other concern is that sex education is being taught like any other textbook course. There is no give and take, no interchange of ideas, no discussion. It's just another lecture—and then the bell rings. What I would like to see is more teacher-student involvement with each other. And what would be wrong with bringing a practicing physician and other experts into the classroom?

*Q. Are you talking about sex education at the high school or grammar school level?*

Ignorance has no place at any level. At the latest, these courses should begin by the fourth grade. Many of the problems we're encountering in our offices today are those of ignorance, and the ignorance is abysmal. It's incredible that, with so much information available at local libraries, people just don't go and ask for it, adults as well as children.

It reminds me of the story of the two high schoolers, during summer vacation, who were reflecting back on the school year. One said, "Did you learn a lot in Mr. Jones' sex ed classes?" And the other replied, "I learned more at recess." By the time many children reach school age, they have already picked up misconceptions, prejudices, and negative attitudes regarding sex from their homes. The impact of sex education in school is overestimated.

*Q. As a mother, I disagree with you completely. I think sex education in school is too explicit. Everything is laid out, which stimulates and encourages the kids to experiment. Our children are not learning to say "no," because they don't know that "no" is a right answer.*

First, you, as a parent, have the right to refuse permission for your child to attend these classes. If you allow your child to participate, you then should make yourself aware of what is being taught in that classroom.

Be accessible to answer any questions that come up. Encourage these questions. If information is given that is not wanted or needed, it will be ignored. Don't give your child a book on the "Birds and the Bees" like my Dad gave me. These developing young people have the right to know what to expect in life, and you have the responsibility of training your children for life. Most children put a lot of faith in their parents' beliefs and are influenced by them.

*Q. As a parent opposed to sex education in schools, how does one fight the peer pressure? If all my youngster's friends are in the class, I can't keep mine out.*

I hear you, and I sympathize with you. But morality is within yourself, your home environment, and what you instill in your child. A lot depends on how you were conditioned by your own background and training. If you had hang-ups, you must bend over backward not to pass them along to the next generation.

I agree that today's morality is very loose, and I decry the influence of the media on our young people. However, it eventually reverts back to you, as a parent.

*Q. What's a parent to do?*

More than you're doing now. Why is it that the teenage counseling clinics report that the vast majority of young people who come to them feel they cannot communicate with their parents?

That means that a lot of *you* have closed down those lines of communication. Perhaps the educators can cover specific information about sexual behavior, venereal disease, contraception, and pregnancy, but what about the human emotions and feelings? Don't those subjects belong to you, within the home? Present the facts of life simply and directly. Parents have an obligation to learn how to play their roles as the primary sex educators. Your attitudes will certainly be conveyed to your children.

*Q. What happened to that old moral adage of a girl "saving herself for marriage"?*

That has almost become a physical impossibility. Puberty today in the female often occurs between the ages of ten and eleven. At the same time, today's young woman is no longer marrying in her late teens. She is often delaying until her middle or late twenties.

Now put yourself in that girl's position, with the peer pressure on one side and her mother's on the other. Add to these pressures her own normal sexual urges. How does she cope as a virginal being between, say, the ages of twelve to twenty-six? She doesn't, of course.

Together with her young man, today's young female may look on sexual activity as a release of tension. If a relationship starts earlier than marriage, might they not begin to learn the "do's and dont's" of human sexuality? You know, an awful lot of divorces are based on sexual incompatibility. So what is worse: early experimentation, or marriage and a doomed relationship, where they are both unhappy and either cheating on or sharpshooting at one another? And what of the children of such a marriage, who may very well be caught in the middle of this rifle range?

*Q. I'm one of those teenage girls who took all the courses and still got pregnant. Sex education is for the birds. They tell you how to do it, but they don't talk to you about feelings. And they don't tell you that you are probably not going to get any satisfaction from the act itself. They don't teach you that a boy only wants one thing, and that he is easily satisfied when a girl is not. They don't tell you that you don't have to do it—that "no" is a viable answer.*

I couldn't have expressed it better. The schools also don't teach enough about conscience and responsibility and the fact that efforts to suppress sexual drives are rarely successful.

But let me say that I see many young men in my office, after their first or second relationship, and they too are truly emotionally disturbed. They don't know what to expect exactly. They don't understand the feelings they have for the girl. They don't know whether they've actually made a commitment to the girl or not. These are responsible young men. They are very upset, and I can't help but believe that their sense of conscience came from their homes, not the schools.

Today, many teenagers first get involved with sex as a challenge: both to society in general and to their parents in particular.

*Q. How do these kids first get involved with sex?*

The same way we did, probably in the back seat of a car. Only today there are more kids and a helluva lot more cars. That first encounter, generally, is not planned. It just sort of happens: "Let's try it and see how we feel."

The big question is "How are they going to feel *later?*" Do our school courses teach them how to deal with that?

Another major problem lies in the fact that the boy has no trouble "getting it off." But, as a lover, on a scale of one to ten he probably rates a good one-half. The girl then starts wondering, "What's wrong with me? I didn't get anything out of that. Maybe I'll try it with another boy, and another."

You can follow this "Is that all there is?" trend for years, right into marriage. Again, a search for a new mate, a new nuclear coupling. Just look at the staggering divorce rate in this land where we have the God-given right for "pursuit of happiness"—whatever that is.

*Q. I can't believe that every teenage boy is on the make and only wants one thing.*

Nor can I. I am seeing many boys now who simply cannot handle this new sexual liberation. Perhaps they were raised in strict, religious homes. Now they are being propositioned by the girls and overwhelmed by how open and forward they are.

At home, the boy might be hearing, "You are much too young to handle anything like this," while, socially, his male friends are saying, "What's wrong with you? There's fun to be had out there," and his girl is explaining, "I'm on the pill, so why not?"

Recently, there has been a deluge of television documentaries dealing with teenage runaways who end up in prostitution. And you'd be amazed how quickly!

Al Palmquist, who is both a clergyman and a police officer in Minneapolis, describes the typical runaway farm girl like this: "As she gets off a bus in Minneapolis, she is immediately propositioned by a pimp, who offers her dinner and instant friendship. Within forty-eight hours, she may very well be out on the streets, as a prostitute" (as told to Owen Spann on radio by Palmquist and Stone). In general, however, teenage girls are more sinned against than sinful.

*Q. I'm a sixteen-year-old boy. And no matter what I hear at home, I feel I am being forced into having sex.*

You probably are. You are being inundated by peer pressures and stimuli. Your friends are saying, "We're doing it. Why aren't you?" You are attending parties where the parents usually are not around. You are living in an age of motorized freedom with your cars and your vans, affording you those weekends at the beach or in ski country. These are your unsure years, the years of exploration and discovery. Use them with discretion. You have a long life ahead.

*Q. But I really don't feel that I want to get into sex. Is there something wrong with me?*

Not at all. You are perfectly normal. Many boys *dread* their first sexual encounter, which usually turns out as an unmitigated disaster. While sexual impulses are instinctive, sexual behavior is only learned through experience.

In your school classes and with your peers, you *are* learning a lot of conflicting things, but you don't know *what* you are learning. For example, I'm sure you don't want to be this year's unwed father, yet most boys expect their girls to be 100 percent responsible for birth control, even though they have never discussed it with them.

*Q. Do you feel any better about advisory social agencies where the kids can go, with or without their parents' knowledge?*

Much better. Let me tell you why. The head of the Planned Parenthood Division of New York's Nassau County said that *90 percent* of the teenagers could *not* tell their parents that they had had intercourse, let alone admit they were pregnant. *90 percent!* (Colton, 1978)

If a fifteen-year-old girl came to her mother for permission to go on the pill, what would be *your* reaction? Some mothers would respond kindly, thanking the Lord that there was enough open communication to allow this conversation to take place. Other parents might react in a "how dare you?" manner and ground the child for weeks.

I think many parents *secretly* thank Planned Parenthood for existing, even though they might not admit their child has been going there. I would certainly like to see more of the techniques of these groups applied to our so-called sex education classes in the schools.

Here is one more disastrous example of how these courses have failed. Last year, there were *three million* new cases of venereal disease, *two-thirds* of which occurred in the under-twenty age group (Crespo, 1978).

In addition to unwanted pregnancies and VD, let me drop in three other depressing consequences of this rampant promiscuity among youth: (1) the highest percentage of high school dropouts occur in this group, (2) the greatest risk of maternal death and infant complications are tied in with teenage pregnancies, and (3) the suicide rate is extremely high. Possibly an influencing factor here is the loss of family support. If a girl finds herself pregnant, her parents' reply is often "You've made your bed—now sleep in it."

*Q. Why would the VD rate be so high if they just "did it" once in the back seat of a car?*

I wish they had done it only once. But they are experimenting more than once, and with more than one partner. And that's a pity, because one out of every four cases of gonorrhea now occurs in adolescents. Every minute of the day, some teenager is getting either gonorrhea or syphilis—at the rate of 500,000 new cases a year.

*Q. Do you feel that all this lurid material available at newsstands adds to the problem?*

*Everything* adds to the problem: lurid material, the media, poor sex education, lack of parental understanding, plus one of the biggest contributors of all—peer pressure.

Look. These kids know *how* to exercise birth control. But they feel that being prepared means taking the spontaneity out of the act. So they gamble. They're considered chicken by their friends unless they go along with this game of Russian Roulette.

The girl who doesn't put out is considered an oddball by the other girls and criticized by the boys, who will find somebody else to take out. So this unusual girl, who wants to be proper, looks around for support. Often it is just not there, especially if sex is a taboo subject in her own home.

Many parents would like to discuss sex openly with their teenagers, but they feel ill at ease and poorly prepared. I've asked pediatricians what their younger patients want to know from them. I was told, "Very little." I've also questioned educators about the inquiries they get after the sex ed classes. Again, almost nothing is asked.

This brings us right back to peer confrontation. In other words, today's youngster is getting advice the same place we all did—from his or her friends. Nothing has changed. They still teach mathematics at Harvard, economics at Stanford, and sex on Main Street.

# Part Two

# *A Man of Parts*

## The Penis

I LOVE THE story about the ten-year-old boy who came home from school and asked his father, "What is a penis?"

The father took him aside, unzipped his fly, showed his son his organ, and said, "This is a penis. And I want you always to remember that it is a *perfect* penis. Look at it carefully."

The next day at school, the son was asked by one of his pals if he had found out what a penis was. Taking his friend aside, the boy unzipped his fly, showed his classmate his organ, and said, "This is a penis. But it's not a perfect penis. To be perfect, it would have to be four inches shorter."

I can think of no part of the human anatomy that evokes more questions, doubts, fantasies, and traumas than the penis. Is it long enough? Is it thick enough? How do *I* compare with the average guy?

From the age of three on, men *and* women retain an absolute fascination with the male member. A man in his fifties, who had a rather large potbelly, complained to me recently that he thought his penis was rapidly getting smaller. What was really happening, of course, was that he couldn't see his penis for his paunch. His penis had remained the same, but the rest of his body hadn't. I suggested that he diet. In all seriousness, he replied, "What color?"

Is it long enough? Is it thick enough? The depth of penetration has nothing to do with providing your mate sexual satisfaction, nor does the width of your penis within her vagina, since vaginal stimulation plays little part in the female satisfaction.

The only question you should be concerned about is: Is it *hard* enough? It is the firmness that counts. If the penis becomes firm during erection, it will stimulate the female clitoris. It's as simple as that.

How do you compare with the average man? The average penis (during erection) is six inches long. Longer or shorter makes *extremely* little difference, or none.

*Q. Do you mean there is no such thing as an undersized penis?*

It does occur rarely in, perhaps, one male out of 100,000. The technical name is *microphallus,* and it is possible to spot it in small children. It could be an hereditary problem involving a group of diseases that you have probably never heard of, but which result in very small penile proportions, both in length and width. The testes are smaller, too (Allen, 1977).

There are some hormone creams, containing testosterone, a male hormone, that can be rubbed directly on the penis. Some of these creams don't work because they are not *absorbed* well enough. The most effective creams incorporate DMSO, dimethyl sulfoxide, a wood pulp extract that enables the medication to penetrate deeply. There *has* been striking response to this therapy. In the younger age group, around ten, it is not unusual to see the penis double in size in as short a time as three months.

In a child, it is also possible to inject pituitary hormones, which will bring on an early puberty. If the child does end up in adult life with an infantile penis, there are any number of implants that can be put inside the penis to stretch it out.

*Q. I may have the reverse problem with regard to penile size. I seem to have too much at the wrong times. I have too many erections. This can get embarrassing, especially in the locker room. Is there anything that can be done medically or surgically to inhibit me some?*

There could be a couple of things wrong. You should have the inside of your urinary passageway examined by means of a lighted instrument, called a *cystoscope*, to inspect the back of your canal in the regions from which you ejaculate. If you have inflammatory tissue there, minimal stimulation may very well result in frequent erections. And I'm talking about even the stimulation of your clothes rubbing on the tip of your penis.

The other problem could be an inflammation of your prostate gland. This can be checked rectally by your doctor, who can massage fluid from the prostate gland and examine it.

I would certainly *not* recommend any procedure that would stop you from having these erections. Many of us would leave well enough alone and be the envy of our neighborhoods.

*Q. For those of us in the service, I've always heard they put saltpeter in our food to keep us from having erections. Is saltpeter effective?*

It certainly is—as a food preservative or in the manufacture of gunpowder, back in early times. But, as an antiaphrodisiac, I seriously doubt it.

Back in the seventeenth century, the Dutch came up with some interesting medical theories. They felt that if sexual excitement was equated with heat, then saltpeter (potassium nitrite), by cooling the blood, would also cool down man's passion. However, they couldn't demonstrate any actual lowering of the body temperature. Saltpeter does tend to increase one's urine flow, but it has no effect on sexual interest or potency.

I have spent considerable time in the service, and I have never been able to find out if such an additive was ever put in the food. This is an old Army-Navy myth and is not detailed in any book on pharmacology. In fact, as most of us think back to our active service days, I would bet we happily recall one erection after another.

*Q. I hear so many men complaining that their penis is too short or too long. My problem is different. Mine is crooked. It goes out at an angle.*

You probably have the *bent spike disease*, and it's not at all unusual. The medical term is Peyronie's disease.

It has to do with the formation of scar tissue in the top part of the penis. The penis has three main channels in it. One carries urine. The other two carry blood.

When these latter two are full, they cause the penis to become rigid or erect. Between these two blood channels, there is a fibrous band of tissue. This tissue can get scarred, either by a local trauma or by a tendency of the person to form scars. So, after much usage, instead of erecting uniformly the penis erects in sort of a cockeyed fashion, at an angle.

There is another situation that can cause the bent spike problem, where no scarring has occurred. Here, one blood-bearing channel might be more developed than the one on the opposite side.

*Q. But there must be some way to straighten out the bent spike?*

Yes. In the latter situation, where there is no scarring, they can take a very fine needle and inject a dye, that will show up on X rays, into the blood-bearing area of the penis and get a picture of the interior of that region to determine the causative factors. Surgery may be indicated, to shorten one side and elongate the other.

As far as Peyronie's disease goes, there are two approaches available. One is an oral medication that can be used in conjunction with vitamin E to counteract the fibrosis. However, if the angulation at the time of erection is so painful that the penis is no longer functional, this band can be surgically removed and a skin graft put in its place to straighten out the penis.

*Q. For the man who can't get an erection, I read that it is possible to build up the penis through the use of a splint. Under what circumstances might this be used?*

There are many such devices available. But to answer your question —under what circumstances—let's review the causes of impotence.

The man with *primary* impotence has *never* been able to get it up. Perhaps he has been caught masturbating, or he may have been turned off by seeing his parents make love—whatever. This fellow will usually respond to psychotherapy, but he is in the minority.

Most men have *secondary* impotence. These are the men who were always able to have relationships but can no longer do so regularly. This group can usually be aided by medication or therapy, after we check out other factors in their lives: tension on the job, overdoses of aspirin (which can interrupt an adequate erection), too many tranquilizers or sedatives, or alcohol. All of these factors can help in creating secondary impotence. Our patient may be going through the first stages of diabetes; and 49 percent of this group will have problems in getting erections.

After checking out all this, there will still be a small percentage of individuals who have a situation we simply cannot correct. Maybe there has been an interruption of the nerve or blood vessel supply to the penis, such as a sympathectomy for hypertension or a bypass operation for advanced arteriosclerosis of the main blood vessels of the body.

Other patients in this category include those people who have had extensive radiation therapy to their lower body, those with multiple sclerosis, and those with spinal cord problems that might have followed injuries. These men will not benefit from any medication or psychother-apy, so an artificial means of creating an erection must be used.

*Q. What kind of artificial devices are available?*

First, you could use a penile cradle that surrounds the penis. The penis rests in it, and it is put on like a dildo, prior to intercourse. Or a doctor can surgically insert a pair of splints into the penis. These are usually made of siliconized rubber and are permanent.

Dr. Brantley Scott at Baylor University has devised an inflatable apparatus that adds a third "ball" to your scrotum. When you squeeze this appendage, you pump fluid from an abdominal reservoir into hollow cylinders that have been implanted in the penis. Thus you can create an erection on demand, whenever you want.

Back to the less extreme options, you can also wear a rigid sheath or condom, that is available today in "head" shops.

And while you're there, you might look over the dazzling display of cock rings. A cock ring is a new variation on the old theme of tightening a rubber band around the base of your penis. The idea is to trap blood in the penis and create an erection. The rubber band idea still works fine, but the current model year now offers you cock rings in leather or plastic, in rubber or metal, and with or without studs (for after-five formal wear?).

*Q. That second choice you mentioned, having a splint permanently put in your penis—wouldn't you be walking around with an erection all the time?*

That is the most common question asked. Most of the splints are flexible and made with a soft piece of material, rubber or silicone, and placed under the arch of the bone where the base of your penis is. Think of it as a long banana, hinged at the base, going from beneath the head of the penis up under the arch of the bone at the base of your penis. It is fastened at that point with a wishbone-type arrangment, so that it can't twist once it is implanted and go wandering around.

Now, to get back to your question, you would usually wear an athletic supporter with your penis turned upward on to your abdomen. Otherwise, yes, you would always be walking around with a semierection.

*Q. Wouldn't the splint be uncomfortable, being there forever and ever?*

There is no discomfort at all. And speaking of "forever," if you ever want it removed and if your original condition improves, the implant can be taken out.

*Q. What kind of money are we talking about for these devices?*

The splint implants cost about $400 for the pair. The surgery is relatively simple, and the hospital stay is short.

The inflatable cylinders are produced in Minnesota. Until recently, the firm sent its own engineer right into the operating room to supervise the procedure and test the apparatus. This ran about $1,800, plus surgeon's fees and hospital costs. This is a very big deal; the whole thing could cost in the neighborhood of $6,000.

Even with these high costs, we cannot absolutely guarantee perfect results, because of the possibilities of infection and body rejection. The complication rate for the splint is 10 percent. For the inflatable cylinders, it is 30 percent, due to fluid leakage from the many plastic connection joints.

*Q. Are these just devices to enable a man to make penetration and please his partner? Does he, himself, get a sexual release? Does he achieve ejaculation? Or is he just buying himself a very expensive long stick?*

Yes. Yes. Yes. Yes.

Such a device enables a man to make penetration. After all, the reason he has gone through all this is to gratify his partner. However, he pleases himself as well. He may or may not achieve an ejaculation, but as a sexually functioning male, his self-esteem is restored.

*Q. I've got a lot of pimples all over my penis. I can squeeze them and a white mucus comes out. My doctor gave me a complete physical, including a prostate exam, and assured me there is nothing wrong. He said I shouldn't worry about the pimples.*

When a man touches himself in the genital area, especially when it is warm, he will notice that his scrotum and his penis have an oily, sticky touch to them. This is caused by the lubricating glands in that area. If these glands get sealed over by a little surface irritation while continuing to produce this oily substance, in time the fluid element of the oil begins to be reabsorbed back into the body. What is left is a thick, cheesy substance which forms whitish bumps under the skin.

These are called *sebaceous cysts.* If they get sore or inflamed, they should be opened. If they don't bother you, leave them alone.

Be sure to wash your genital area at least two or three times a *day* with an unscented soap, preferably containing hexachloraphene. Also, use a lot of baby talcum powder to keep the area dry by absorbing skin moisture and oil.

# The Testes

Years ago, J. D. Ratcliff (1970, 1971, 1972, 1974) did a whole series of articles for *Reader's Digest* entitled "I am Joe's Liver," "I am Joe's Bladder," and so on. To show you how far our society has come in just a few years, let me quote a few lines from Ratcliff's November 1970 story called "I am Joe's Man Gland": "There are two of me. I manufacture 50 million sperm cells a day. *Every two months,* I produce cells that have the potential of populating *the entire earth.*" (Good Lord! If the Zero Population Growth people ever get hold of Joe, they'll probably string him up.) Seriously, even back in 1970, did you ever catch yourself referring to your testicles as your "man glands"? Probably you used words like *balls* and *nuts,* didn't you? Or phrases like "That guy doesn't have the balls to swing that business deal" or "She's so tough she must have balls."

Through the years, the words *balls, testicles,* or *nuts* have become equated with courage, guts, and masculinity.

One explanation would take us back to the childhood fear of castration, where the young boy learns that his female counterpart doesn't have any balls; and he worries that his are going to fall off.

The neutered male animal has been held up to ridicule, or why did Ferdinand the Bull really prefer smelling flowers? Once it is castrated, society looks on it as a passive creature, lacking aggressiveness.

Does the same thing hold true for a man? Are his testes the symbol of his masculinity? Yes, the answer lies in what the testes actually do. The primary function of the testes is to produce male hormone, called *testosterone*, which influences all the secondary male sex characteristics, such as hair growth, skin oil production, pitch of voice, muscular development, and behavior patterns, especially those related to sex. Testosterone enters the body from the testes through the bloodstream. The levels of this hormone vary greatly in each man, even within a single day, depending on stress, activity, and whether he's awake or asleep.

The second function of the testes is to produce sperm. Without them, you can never become a daddy, which brings us right back to where we started: balls, nuts, and testes *do* equate with masculinity.

*Q. Since everybody seems so interested in how large or how small their testes are, what is the normal size?*

I'll have to give it to you in the metric system, as medicine has pioneered this great new trend in American mathematics.

The normal testicle is, roughly, 2.5 centimeters across and 3 to 4 centimeters in length. (There are about 2.5 centimeters to the inch.) Now, this can vary according to body size. Usually, the bigger the man, the bigger the testicles.

*Q. Can mumps or scarlet fever in a young boy cause problems in later life?*

Fortunately, neither disease is that common anymore. However, if a high fever accompanied the illness, the heat of the body could cause sperm production problems later on.

With mumps, a painful swelling of the testes as well as the facial glands in front of the ears may occur. This virus infection causes the swollen testes to push against their strong covers, destroying the delicate tissues in which sperm develop. The result could be sterility. After this infectious disease subsides, the testes often shrink, due to extensive tissue destruction.

Under certain conditions, the testicles can be very small from birth because of an endocrine disease. One such disease is called Klinefelter's Syndrome, in which not enough male hormone is produced. The result of this is decreased fertility and sexual inactivity. George Washington suffered from this problem. Today, the patient's own hormones can be supplemented by hormone injections, but not in George Washington's day. Let me put it this way. He may have been the father of our country, but he was *not* the father of Martha's kids.

*Q. As a young man, I recall being sexually frustrated by a girl who refused to go "all the way." Then I would get this terrible pain, which we called "lovers' nuts." What was really happening in my body?*

Ah, you bring back terrible memories of the not-so-golden times of our youth. I'm sure each of us can recall being barely able to walk home at night, doubled over from a case of "lovers' nuts" or "blue balls."

When a man is aroused, blood vessel congestion builds up in the penis and in the prostate. The glands are crying for ejaculatory release. When this does not occur, this congestion persists, and one is left temporarily disabled, not even eligible for workman's compensation.

This condition will spontaneously subside by either taking a cold shower or masturbating. Unless you get yourself into this situation over and over again, "lovers' nuts" are harmless. Not pleasant, but harmless.

*Q. I developed a terrible pain in my testicle last month. My doctor told me it was twisted. What does this mean?*

The testes are paired, egg-shaped organs, regular in outline, which hang like cherries on the end of a stem, within the scrotal sac. The stem consists of blood vessels and nerves. If a testicle turns within the sac, the blood supply is blocked off. Sudden, acute pain and swelling follow. It can happen to any man at any age, during a period of activity or inactivity.

The treatment indicated is to untwist the kink in the stem, and quickly, before the testis is lost due to lack of blood flow. The easiest approach is to turn the testicle back to its original position. Unhappily, it doesn't always stay there. If that's the case, open surgery is required, not only to untwist the stem but also to fix the testicle in its proper position.

*Q. I am fifty years old. About ten years ago, I had an accident. I fell off a truck, straddled a two-by-four, and split a testicle. Where it split, another one grew. I have three now. My doctor said not to worry, but I am having some pain down there.*

If I might be allowed a humorous moment, you could go into the pawn shop business.

What has probably happened is that you have an unresolved clot, or hematoma. The remnants of the testicle that split gives you the *feeling* of three objects in your sac. If it is causing you pain, I would have it removed. You are producing adequate hormones on the opposite side, so the surgery will not affect your love life. There is a chance that your fertility could be reduced, but at your age that is probably not a major concern.

*Q. I developed a swelling near my left testicle. It's become very inflamed and painful. Is there anything I can do about it?*

When you are naked, you'll notice that your left testicle is usually lower than your right. That's because the blood vessels on the left side are longer, going up into the body, than those on the right side. Therefore, blood tends to puddle on the left side. If you feel the bottom of your scrotum, you'll notice that it has the sensation of a bag of worms. These are enlarged veins called a *varicocele;* not an uncommon situation.

This condition can also be brought on by straining when you are moving your bowels or by standing a great deal without scrotal support. Try a jock strap first. If that doesn't give you relief, a physician can tie off these varicose veins through a very small incision in the abdomen.

If it's not bothering you that much, live with it and don't be concerned.

*Q. When do the testes come down? We have a seven-year-old son with both of them undescended. What should we do?*

A baby is usually born with both testes descended, or they drop shortly thereafter. This should have already occurred in your son. If both testes are absent, a hormonal deficiency is probably indicated.

Physicians are most concerned about a case like this, for several reasons. First, the abdomen is three degrees warmer than the scrotum. Even at the age of five, the basic cells for creating sperm are being formed, and this increased heat interferes with sperm production by the testes. And, secondly, there is a greater incidence of cancer in undescended testes.

Your son's condition would suggest one of two immediate approaches: large hormone injections over a short period of time, or, if the injections are ineffective, immediate surgery to bring the testes down.

*Q. If surgery is indicated, is that a major operation on a child?*

Any surgery on a child is a major undertaking. The extent depends upon where the testes are located. After making a cut in the groin, we would try to free up any scar tissue binding the cord and testicle. The object here is to make the cord longer, so that the testicle may be deposited in its normal position within the scrotum. If there just isn't enough cord available, the testis should be removed. This would be the case when the testis is found within the abdomen rather than lower in the groin.

*Q. If the testicles never do descend, or if a man is born without them, is it possible to transplant a healthy testicle from a donor?*

We may be on the verge of a breakthrough here for very specific situations. In St. Louis, Dr. Sherman Silber performed the first successful human testicle transplant in August 1978. This operation involved identical twin brothers, one of whom was born with two testicles and the other with none. The recipient, thirty years old, is now fertile and potent enough to father children.

So far, the operation is restricted to identical twins, because of the danger of organ rejection. Hopefully, in the future, a father might be able to donate a testicle to his son. It is still a very complicated microsurgical procedure.

*Q. Are there men born with just one testicle?*

Yes, and this isn't nearly as important as being born without any, since the one descended testicle may take over the total function of fertility. In a case like this, if there is trouble, it is more likely to be mechanical rather than hormonal. We commonly see this condition occur where the baby is born with a hernia, blocking his groin canal thus preventing a normal testicle from dropping into the scrotum. Surgical repair is indicated before the age of five, since hormonal therapy will be ineffective.

*Q. Can anything be done for an adult male if one of his testicles has slipped back up into his body?*

We call this a *hyperactive reflex,* or the *male defense mechanism.*

I think every man can remember getting scared, really scared. For example, you may have had a near miss in your car on the highway and averted a crash by slamming on the brakes. Then, a few moments later, you may have found yourself shaking and sweating. I'll admit, at that instant, very few men would wonder what was happening to their testes during that period. Men with hyperactive muscles might find themselves pulling their testicles right up into the canal during a "crisis"—or during love making, as a matter of fact. In cold weather the scrotal sac appears to shrink as a means of body heat conservation.

There are two loops of muscles, one on each side, called the *cremaster* muscles. They come up from within the abdomen and go around the testicle. During sexual excitment and ejaculation, they tend to tighten up and pull up within your body. So it appears that your testes, or one of them, are shrinking in size.

This is not abnormal at all. If you want to snap back into shape after testis retraction, massage yourself with a warm cloth, or a warm hand, starting at the waistline and working down toward the scrotal sac.

If this condition causes you pain, the only surgical answer would be to cut the loop of muscle that comes down over the testicle. It would lessen your defense mechanism, but most of us keep ourselves pretty well guarded in that area anyway.

*Q. Every year when I get my physical, the doctor always asks me to "drop my pants." Then he takes hold of my testicles and asks me to turn my head and cough. What's this all about?*

We instruct you to turn your head sideways simply because we don't want you coughing on *us.* If you looked for a deeper medical explanation, there just isn't any.

As to the cough itself, we want to increase the pressure within your abdomen. You could get the same reaction by straining down, as if moving your bowels.

Here's what we are looking for. The testicles descend from the body, just about the time of birth, through a tiny canal that is part of the lining membrane of the interior part of the body. It's called the *peritoneum*. This membrane dries up during birth or shortly thereafter.

If the membrane stays open, a weakness develops in that canal where the testicle is descending. Three muscles cross this area and form a triangle. When the muscles are not quite as solid as they should be, you can get a protrusion of the lining membrane, or the peritoneum, which may contain intestine.

This is a hernia or rupture. What your doctor is testing you for is to see whether or not you have a weakness along this canal, indicating an actual or potential hernia.

*Q. If you find this condition, what have you actually found? What is a hernia?*

A hernia is a blowout. Picture it this way: Puff up one cheek; the bulge that shows is a hernia.

The same thing occurs along your spermatic canal. Because of those weak muscles I mentioned, the lining membrane of the body, the peritoneum, protrudes along the spermatic cord. This bulge may contain a loop of intestine. If this loop gets trapped, it is called a *strangulated* hernia and requires immediate repair.

Your doctor will replace the intestine in its normal position. He will then cut out the hernia sac, sew up the lining membrane, and pull the abdominal muscles together.

Although this may sound complicated, it represents a fantastic step forward from a generation ago, when a hernia sufferer had to constantly wear a truss—a rigid belt that was fitted with a large pad.

*Q. Since that test for a hernia is a routine part of a yearly physical exam, does that mean it can develop gradually, or does it come on suddenly?*

Either. Let me explain. Many men have wide canals but not hernias. These men are more subject to developing hernias, particularly with sudden or unaccustomed exertion. Picking up a heavy object can cause an *instant* hernia. The muscles tear, the bulge protrudes, and you've got it. That heavy object story is not just an old husband's tale.

Hernias may also develop slowly as the muscular reinforcements tend to spread apart. This is a gradual process that may not be related to any specific exertion. Your doctor can notice these changes through the years.

*Q. Recently my testicles seem to have enlarged to the point where my shorts no longer fit me. I also have a heavy sensation in my groin. What's going on?*

You probably have a water sac, or *hydrocele.* This is an accumulation of fluid around the testicle or spermatic cord, usually resulting from an inflammation of the testicle or from the small gland sitting above it. It can be treated either by drawing off the fluid with a needle and syringe, or by surgically removing the water sac.

*Q. The Cancer Society keeps urging women to examine their breasts for possible tumors. Is there any similar thing a man can do?*

You bet. In this age of preventive medicine, a self-examination of the "family jewels" is just as important to men as the breast examination is for women.

I *urge* all men to examine their *testes* monthly. The best time to do it is when you are standing in the shower, as they are easily available for inspection. First off, have you got *two?* Are they oval and about the consistency of Jello? Feel them from the top. Don't be afraid—press down on them. Are there any abnormal lumps or painful areas?

Unhappily, many cancers of the testes lie within the mass of the testicle itself. So the only thing you can feel is a difference in the firmness of the organ. Cancer of the testes is not a major disease, in that its incidence rate is less than 1 percent of all male malignancies. It most frequently occurs in men in their thirties and usually presents no symptoms, but it is a terrible cancer. Unless you find it early, you've lost the patient.

Where we do find a higher rate of cancer is in the undescended testicle. Here you have a *thirty* times greater incidence.

*Q. If a man has been castrated, either through an accident or for medical reasons, I realize he can no longer have children. But can he enjoy any sex life at all?*

He certainly can, since sex is a learned act. As an adult, he has probably already learned it.

Timing is the major factor here. Castration is the removal of the testes. If this occurred in a young boy, prior to puberty, he would have no learned reflex to fall back on in order to have an erection. This was what was done to the eunuchs who served the sultans' harems in olden days.

However, castration after puberty should not result in any loss of erectile ability. Many adult men, castrated through surgery or injury, are still able to function sexually.

The fluid element of your ejaculate comes from the prostate gland. Only one or two drops come up from the testes. So when ejaculation occurs, the castrated male has the same amount of fluid, but there are no sperm in it.

*Q. I thought I read that eunuchs weren't harmless at all but actually serviced the ladies of the harem?*

You're right, the sultan was only *one* man, who could hardly *be* everywhere and *do* everything by himself.

The eunuchs castrated *after* puberty, were, indeed, used to service the harem, harmlessly. They still had the learned reflex and ejaculate but no sperm. You have another source of testosterone in the body from the adrenal glands, so there is enough secondary production of testosterone for you to have an erection on the basis of that production.

Let me destroy one other fallacy—that castration would bring out all kinds of feminine characteristics, including a high-pitched voice. It just isn't true. Your voice box has deepened after you reach puberty, and your voice muscles are set for life. Even in the sex-change operations—male to female, for example—we can change the patient's body, but not the voice.

# The Prostate Gland

Why is it that the average man will refer to this most important part of his anatomy as his PROS*TRATE?* A PROS*TRATE* condition would be one in which somebody just hit you over the head with a two-by-four; and you're stretched out on the ground—PROS*TRATE*. Nothing is further from being *out* of it than your PROS*TATE.* This is where the *action* is.

At the height of your sexual ecstasy, when your ejaculate spurts out of your penis, it comes from your prostate. When you feel that warm, familiar swelling in your penis, your prostate is responsible.

The prostate is actually a group of glands that, together, are about the size of a large chestnut. Its location is below the bladder at the top of the urinary passageway.

Let me try to describe it a little better for you. Think of the bladder as a child's balloon, with a long nozzle. The balloon represents the bladder; the nozzle represents your urinary passageway. If you tied a string around the nozzle, you would usually tie it right where the nozzle comes off the balloon, at the beginning of the urinary passageway. That's where the prostate is, surrounding the base of the nozzle.

In a newborn baby, the prostate is no bigger than a kernel of rice. It remains that way until puberty, when the male hormone flow surges. That's when the prostate comes into its own. At that point, the pituitary growth factor changes over to stimulate the production of sperm. Can't you just hear the pituitary saying, "OK, prostate, I've done all I can for *you*. Now I've got to get that old sperm started."

What is the function of the prostate? It makes 99 percent of the ejaculate fluid and the enzymes that activate sperm. Only 1 percent of the fluid comes from the testicles.

Now let's put the whole thing together. The sperm, in a state of suspended animation, are delivered up to the reservoir in back of the prostate gland. At the time of ejaculation, they get activated or nourished by enzymes in the prostate fluid. The sperm are delivered through ducts in the gland that run forward in direction, expelling the fluid out through the penis.

Now that you realize the importance of this group of glands, pronounce it right the next time: Pro*state*.

*Q. So far, you've talked about the neat things the prostate does, helping with ejaculations and erections. I'm in my thirties. What can go wrong?*

In your age group, the most common complaint is prostatitis or prostatosis. And complain you would: of a dragging sensation in your low back and pain on the underside of your body between the scrotum and the rectum when you sit. Prostatosis may be due to an inflammation from fatigue, if your resistance is low, if you are chilled, or if you have a zinc deficiency. You can also develop this problem if your prostatic fluid is retained. This fluid deteriorates and causes congestion within the glands, a situation commonly seen among celibate members of the clergy. It is also known as "truck driver's" or "motorcyclist's disease," because of the constant irritation of the underside of the body. The sexually *over*active male is also prone to this disorder, since he is overworking his prostate.

Prostatitis is usually caused by a bacterial infection, from the rectum, through the bloodstream or from infected urine. The only difference between these two conditions is the presence or absence of bacteria.

*Q. What is meant by an enlarged prostate? Is something like this going to happen to most of us in later life?*

Not necessarily. In the first place, age can be deceiving. Chronological age and body age are not always the same thing. A man can be old at forty or young at seventy-five.

As you grow older, you may get an enlarged prostate. The odds increase right along with your age: at age sixty, 60 percent chance, at age seventy, 70 percent, and so on. We have found no hereditary factors in men who have prostate problems. Whether or not your father had an enlarged prostate has no bearing on you.

Why does it get bigger? The gland itself may not be getting bigger. But within the gland small benign tumors, similar to the fibroid growths in women, develop. Although 75 percent of these are not malignant, they can still lead to serious trouble.

*Q. What are the symptoms of an enlarged prostate?*

About half of the men involved here will have *no* symptoms. But there are some danger signs to look for that may gradually develop.

You find yourself urinating differently. Your stream may be slower. You may get up at night more frequently, and even after urinating your bladder still may feel full. You may find that, even when you have the urge to go, you have to wait and wait even to get a scanty flow started. You may get to the point where you cannot urinate at all. This is called *acute urinary retention,* which could lead to uremic poisoning and kidney failure.

This situation requires instant relief, usually with a doctor inserting a catheter through the penis to permit drainage of the bladder.

*Q. Wait a minute. Doesn't every man find himself getting up more often at night as he gets older?*

Yes. The odds go up with your age, and you get up more in the night. But if that's your only symptom it doesn't mean you have any problems.

As a man gets older, other thoughts and worries intrude. He may be a light sleeper, so that the slightest noise disturbs him. Since it takes several hours for fluid to clear from his system, drinking too many liquids while watching evening television or attending an evening dinner function may cause him to produce urine more rapidly during those early sleeping hours, with an increased urge to urinate. If a partial obstruction has been starting and has been present over a period of years, his bladder wall will be trying hard to push urine through the smaller opening. The bladder wall will thicken and thereby decrease capacity. So his bladder may simply be filling more frequently to near capacity, giving him the urge to arise more frequently at night.

*Q. Let's say I fit too many of your danger signs. How does a doctor tell if I actually do have serious prostate problems?*

I hope you have an annual physical examination and that a rectal evaluation is part of it. Remember when your doctor asks you to bend over and bear down? That's when he puts his index finger into your rectum and feels along the front wall to determine the shape and size of your prostate gland. If it is smooth, don't worry. If it is bumpy, worry. Your doctor will know fast enough.

Secondly, a simple blood test will see if the enzymes from your prostate are abnormal. Your physician might also inject a dye in your arm and take X rays of your kidney, bladder, and prostate to determine how well they are functioning. And, finally, he might pass a rubber tube (catheter) through your penis to measure how much urine you are holding back and how much obstruction exists.

*Q. Why do doctors refer to an examination of the prostate as a "prostate massage"?* The word *massage* sounds so gentle, but that examination is just awful.

I agree that words can be deceiving. It is like when your garage mechanic suggests you need a "tune-up." The word tune-up also sounds gentle until you get a bill for $600 after they have rebuilt your entire engine.

What would you suggest? Should we call it a "finger wave," "prostate manipulation," or a "prostate feeling-around"? It is still going to hurt just as much, but only for a little while.

I will admit this is the part I, myself, dread most in *my* annual checkup, when I am asked to bend over and spread my cheeks. The next time you have to have this done, help your doctor. If you bear down, the entrance of his finger is made much easier. Actually, he *is* massaging the two biggest lobes of the gland. He massages from the outside to the middle on one side, then the other. Then he strips all the fluid that you are expressing down the center of the gland. That is when you get a searing pain going through your penis.

If you want to be of aid to your physician at this point, please don't waggle your tail, or he could very easily injure his examining finger. This might give *you* pleasure but put *him* out of commission.

*Q. Is there anything a man can do in his middle years to prevent prostate enlargement in later life?*

Stay young! Now, I know that sounds ridiculous. We all want to do that. But I like to get my patients into any exercise that will increase blood circulation around the pelvic area—the area between your hips. The best for this is bicycle riding, because you tend to flex your hips up and down rather vigorously. This can be done on a real bicycle, an exercycle, or just phantom bicycling lying on the floor at home.

Another good way to decongest the prostate area is by frequent swimming, hot tub bathing or whirlpools.

The third recommendation is a regular sex life, because you evacuate the prostate fluid regularly every time you ejaculate. I don't think men should cut down on their frequency of intercourse as they get older, feeling maybe that's the way it's supposed to be. Do what comes naturally. If you have the urge, go to it.

*Q. Let's say the checkup has shown that I do have an enlarged prostate and I am retaining urine. What's the next step?*

You're probably going to need surgery, to remove the obstruction. Please understand that we simply remove the growth, not the prostate itself.

There are three major ways to go. The most popular procedure is called a *transurethral resection* (TUR) and is performed through the penis. This is the so-called ream job or roto-rooter technique. The surgeon looks into the urinary passageway through a lighted magnifying telescope. Then, under direct vision, he is able to scoop out the growth with an electric wire loop.

The second most popular method is called a *retropubic approach.* Here, a cut is made in your lower belly to permit the surgeon to go behind the pubic bone and directly down on the prostate area. After opening the gland, he scoops out the obstructive tissue.

The third approach, which is rarely used any longer except in extreme cases, is called a *perineal approach.* An incision is made between the scrotum and rectum on the underside of the body and the prostatic growth is removed from below. This technique has fallen out of favor because it is associated with a very high rate of impotence.

*Q. What are the aftereffects of prostatic surgery?*

It will often render the individual sterile, because the sperm duct is frequently cut across or scarred. He may find, when he ejaculates, that the fluid goes *backward* into the bladder rather than out through the tip of his penis. He will still have all the sensations of orgasm but may experience a total or partial dry run.

Remember, sterility does not mean impotence. After prostatic surgery, he should be just as competent sexually as before, if not better!

That reminds me of the story about the man who asks his doctor after prostate surgery how soon he can drive his car, and the doctor after thinking a moment says, "Well, I think you ought to be able to drive in about a week," to which the patient replies, "That's wonderful Doc, I don't even have a license." So if you were sexually active before your surgery, you'll be just as good afterwards.

*Q. I had a TUR about a year ago. I still don't understand why I am ejaculating backward.*

Picture a hallway with two swinging doors. The inner door opens easily; the outer door does not. These doors represent the valves that control urinary flow. TUR surgery is done *between* these valves, resulting in some weakening of the inner section. When ejaculation occurs, the fluid may follow the path of least resistance, through the weaker valve, back into the bladder. In fact, after TUR surgery, you can frequently recover sperm from the urine in cases like yours.

*Q. Several years ago, I had a prostate operation, the one through the penis. Now I've become sore in at least three places: on the underside of the head of the penis, a dull scrotal pain somewhat like a stone ache, and a pain in the pubic hair area itself.*

There may be a definite relationship between these three symptoms. On the underside of the head of the penis, I suspect that you have a little scar tissue, which was brought about by the use of the instrument in the penis. There are usually five narrowings along the male canal, and the tip of the penis is one of them. With the use of a catheter after a TUR procedure, it's not uncommon for that area to be irritated and further narrowed. You might need a little gentle dilation to take care of that problem.

The pain in the pubic hair area is probably related to inadequate emptying of your bladder. Here, the doctor who did the original surgery can simply stretch the canal.

The stone ache may be caused by a low-grade irritation from not fully evacuating yourself. A drop or two of urine may be going back down your cords to your testes. I think these problems are representative of potential post-TUR complications.

*Q. I seem to have the reverse problem. When I ejaculate, it seems that tons of semen come out. Does this have anything to do with the prostate?*

The amount of semen a man generally ejaculates is somewhere around a teaspoonful, or about 4 to 5 cc in the metric system. Those of you who recall making love four or five times in a single night can remember you started to get drier as the evening wore on. The amount of fluid drops off as the frequency of intercourse increases.

And, yes, the prostate gland is involved. The prostate is spongy in composition. If you squeeze the sponge you drain the fluid out. It then takes a while for the sponge to fill up again. Your problem of excessive semen could indicate that you have more glandular tissue present in the area, or it might signify a mild inflammation where the gland is responding by overproduction of fluid. This condition could dilute the concentration of sperm in your semen, but, unless you're trying to be a poppa, there is probably nothing to worry about.

*Q. I'm sixty-four years old. Two years ago, I had an infection in my prostate. Since then I have had no erections at all. Would this be due to the infection?*

I hardly think so. Perhaps things in general are starting to wane a bit with you. You may have restrained from sexual activity until the infection was over. Again, I go back to my belief of "use it or lose it."

I suggest you get a willing female companion and try some more adequate stimulation. You might also have some hormonal studies done by your family physician. There are other things he can check: anything from an unexpected diabetes to the first sign of multiple sclerosis.

*Q. I am also in my sixties. ʌ have prostate trouble, but I'm trying to put off having an operation. Is there any alternative to surgery?*

Some enzymes are now being used that contain glutamic acid. In certain individuals, these hold some promise in their ability to shrink the prostate. Other enzymes, from banana, papaya, and pineapple peels, have also effected shrinkage by dissolving the swollen tissue. Whether or not it will help *your* prostate condition, I can't guarantee. Some natural food and orthomolecular experts feel that high doses of zinc, magnesium and selenium may help. You can get these in most drugstores or natural food stores. They may work temporarily, but eventually you will probably have to have surgery.

*Q. Is it possible to bleed from the prostate gland and still be in perfect health? I've had X rays and nothing appears to be wrong.*

There probably is nothing wrong. You can bleed from a little varicose vein, which lines the surface of the prostate. You may have strained yourself and knocked some small clots loose. The other area of concern would be the duct from which you ejaculate. This goes through the prostate and ends up in a reservoir behind it. You could tear a blood vessel there without having an infection, and it would have no significance except to worry you.

Now, let me worry you. Bleeding from this area *could* be due to tuberculosis or cancer. I'm not saying they are, but I strongly suggest you see your doctor.

*Q. I thought tuberculosis had to do with the lungs, not the prostate.*

Unhappily, tuberculosis of the genitourinary tract is not uncommon. If I see persistent bleeding with a positive skin test, I might suspect the presence of tuberculosis.

The bacteria can enter this area through the bloodstream. Cultures and smears of the urine and prostatic fluid may reveal the presence or absence of T.B. bacteria. X rays can show characteristic abnormalities, including calcium deposits in the kidneys or prostate area.

*Q. What do you look for if you suspect cancer of the prostate?*

If the gland feels stony hard or bumpy on a rectal examination, the chances are 85 percent that a malignancy is present. In 50 percent of the cases, we find the prostate enzyme (acid phosphatase) elevated.

An X ray of the bony skeleton can reveal abnormal deposits that resemble cotton balls. Here, the chances are better than eight in ten that there is a cancer. We can also ascertain this through the use of radioisotope dye studies.

Our other remaining test is an actual prostatic biopsy. This is an office procedure done under local anesthetic. A long hypodermic needle is inserted into the prostate, either through the wall of the rectum or in the area between the scrotum and the rectal opening. A tiny core of tissue is removed for microscopic examination.

*Q. How common is cancer of the prostate?*

It is rarely seen in the under-forty age group. After the age of fifty-five, cancer of the prostate is the third largest cause of cancer death in men, and 25 percent of all men with an enlarged prostate have this cancer.

*Q. What is the treatment for cancer of the prostate?*

We feel that this type of cancer possibly results from an overproduction of male hormone. Obviously, then, this hormone must be neutralized, either by castration or by administering female hormones. It may be necessary to remove the entire gland, with high risks of urinary incontinence (loss of control) and sexual impotence. Radiation therapy may also be used, either on an internal basis by implanting radioactive gold seeds into the tumor area, or by external radiation through linear accelerator or cobalt units. The type of treament would depend on the type of tumor and its extent.

# The Bladder

How many times have you heard someone say, "I've got to take a leak so bad that my eye teeth are floating and my kidneys are about to burst?"

There are *two* things wrong with that statement: (1) I have never seen a floating canine tooth, and (2) even if your kidneys burst (they don't) it would have nothing to do with taking a leak. The bladder won't burst, either, unless struck when overfilled.

The bladder is a muscular, distendible organ located in the center of your abdomen, right above the pubic hair. It has two functions: to keep urine in and to let urine out. Two sets of muscles control the whole operation. When the bladder wall contracts to push urine out, the bladder neck opens. When the bladder neck closes to keep you from dripping, the bladder wall relaxes.

Push, pull, click, click. Most of the time it works just fine.

*Q. When I get the urge to urinate, it's almost too late then. I mean, when I have to go, I have to go, right that minute.*

You could have several problems. We must first consider urgent urination, or precipitancy. Is your urine irritating your bladder? Is your bladder capacity so low that a small amount of urine fills it up quickly to the point where it overflows? Is your bladder holding urine back, even though you might be unaware of it?

I'd suggest that you be catheterized to see how much urine is being held back and have a urine study to determine its character. In other words, you might be irritating yourself. While an x-ray examination may give the answer, there is a newer medical technique, called *urodynamics,* that actually measures the bladder capacity and its ability to function. Finally, a cystoscopic examination may be indicated. That involves looking inside the urinary passageway with a lighted telescope.

*Q. You want to look up where, with what?*

The cystoscopic visual examination of the interior of the penis and bladder is done to check out the urinary tract. It's an office procedure, so don't let it terrify you. We use lots of lubrication, a tranquilizer, and a local deadening agent. And more importantly we haven't lost a patient yet.

*Q. Can wet, cold winter weather make us want to "go" more?*

Lots of people become leaky in cold, wet weather, much like your home plumbing.

Every day, the liquids you drink pass through your body. In hot weather, some 50 to 60 percent is lost through your lungs, as vapor and through your skin as perspiration. But in cold weather, this figure drops to 30 percent. That's why your urine output increases. It has to come out somewhere.

Recent studies have shown that in cold weather the pituitary gland produces a hormone which, in turn, increases your urine production.

*Q. Not only do I have to "go" more in winter but I also find myself dripping, unable to control those last few drops.*

Often this leakage is caused by poor muscular action, rather than a loss of control. Muscles in any area of the body, if not regularly exercised, become flabby.

Between the urinary cutoff valve and the tip of the penis, there is a hollow canal, some six to eight inches in length. There are no muscles in this area, so a column of water is often held inside the penis after urination. This may drip out when you put your penis back in your pants. It *is* embarrassing to see this final stream running down your leg and ruining your new pants.

It's a very simple matter to practice starting and stopping your urinary flow. The idea is to contract and relax these muscles around the bladder and rectum. This is the "traffic" exercise—stop and go, stop and go. Try this many times a day, every time you think of it. You'll see a fast improvement.

*Q. What is there about trying to urinate on a cold day at a football game? You're standing at a urinal, and there may be six guys waiting behind you, and you just can't go.*

Many men are simply embarrassed about urinating in public. Add to this the fact that your muscles don't work as well in cold weather. For pressure, throw in those six guys waiting behind you and it is no wonder you find yourself at a dead end.

The urge to pee and the actual valve openings are controlled by two different sets of nerves. While the physical "go" signal may be working from sheer water volume, the emotional "stop" signal won't open the faucet. Go to the back of the line, try to get warmer and work up to it again.

Men should take heart, though. Women also feel this sort of pressure, and they have the additional problem of removing layer after layer of clothing. I had a woman patient who couldn't urinate *anywhere* but in her own home, because she considered every other place *dirty*. If she went away for a weekend at Lake Tahoe, for example, she had to be catheterized in the emergency room at that local hospital. She was a virtual prisoner in her own home, except for quick trips to her local supermarket. Eventually, psychotherapy solved her problem.

*Q. I have that same cold weather hang-up. When the snowflakes start falling, my water freezes up, too. What can I do for antifreeze?*

I'd suggest Prestone mixed with Perrier water, but you might take me seriously.

Actually, cold weather does get your muscles uptight, and, since the antidote for cold is heat, I'd suggest some warm water. I'm sure we all have had the experience of stretching out in a hot tub and suddenly finding ourselves urinating a full stream right in the tub with us and our soapy suds. At that point, we had no control over our bladder. It did what it wanted to.

If a tub isn't available, try soaking one or both hands in warm water or pour warm water over your privates. Just make sure it isn't too warm. If it's too hot to stick your finger in, it's too hot for your penis.

Other people can only "go" if they hear the sound of running water. Such people will open the tap to get themselves started. Running water produces a visual image of a brook and psychologically enables one to babble right along in it.

*Q. Why does a man wake up with a morning erection?*

This is the classic morning situation that men of all ages have experienced. Although people believed for years that this was a reflex caused by a full bladder, we now feel it has more to do with dreaming.

In any given night, four to five involuntary erections will occur, at approximately ninety-minute intervals. This happens during a rapid eye movement (REM) stage, which takes up twenty-five percent of our normal sleeping time.

These are our uninhibited moments of sleep when erotic dreams occur. The morning erection is merely the last of these REM levels. We remember it because that's the one we wake up with. Isn't it a shame we have forgotten the others?

However, you may have a problem putting that morning erection to use, as your sexual mate is hardly conditioned to instantly receive you at that ungodly hour.

*Q. Why is it, when I do get up to pee with a morning erection, almost nothing comes out?*

All this pressure creates a certain amount of swelling in the valve area. In addition, there is the normal congestion of your erect penis. That's why your stream is somewhat reduced when you get up to urinate.

*Q. Why do I find myself getting up to go to the bathroom three or four times a night?*

The fluid you have consumed after dinner—say, from 6 PM to bedtime—plays a big part in this. Fluid has weight, and the average clearance time from your body is three to four hours.

As the fluid accumulates in your bladder, it presses on the valve that controls your water passage, so it is quite common to find yourself getting up around 4 AM to "go."

The most important thing here is to restrict your fluids after dinner. When the movie of the week gives you that five-minute station identification jazz, head for the toilet, not the refrigerator.

*Q. Several years ago, my doctor found that all my canals were small, so he enlarged the opening at the tip of the penis to twice its normal size. Now I urinate in a wide "v," resulting in an inability to hit the urinal. I have to sit down whenever I go, and, frankly, this is quite embarrassing. Can anything be done?*

What you describe is what we call "forking." Your opening is now in the shape of a narrow cleft. The only thing I could suggest to you is to manually open the tip of your penis prior to urination. See if this doesn't help.

*Q. My seven-year-old son is a bed wetter. He has always been a bed wetter. That kid has never had a dry night in his life. What's wrong?*

Your son is probably feeling as bad as you are about this. Socially, he can't go on camping trips or on sleepovers with his friends.

I'd like to know more about your family. Do you have other sons and when were they toilet trained? Did his father have a problem with bed wetting? If this does seem to be a family "tradition," there may be an inherited physical basis, such as overactive valves or a narrow urinary passageway, especially at the tip of the penis. Surgical treatment can help here. Medications to decrease involuntary bladder overactivity are available and may be indicated.

In many instances, I've seen a milk allergy bring on bed wetting. Eliminate liquids after dinner. Encourage your son to urinate twice before bedtime. Wake him up when you go to bed and again in the morning, if you get up before he does. And make his last evening hour before bed a relaxed one. No "Starsky and Hutch."

I personally do not favor wiring him up to alarms and shocks, should he pee in the middle of the night. Emphasize the positive. Plan a reward system for his dry nights and ignore the wet ones.

*Q. Have you ever heard of adult bed wetting? If I have a couple of beers, I can't control myself through the night.*

It's probably not the beer, by itself. The same amount of any liquid would give you the same result.

Again, picture the bladder as an expandable balloon. Over the years, its ability to expand may be diminished by some low-grade irritation, so its capacity is reduced. Once you fall asleep and relax your muscles, after a moderate amount of fluid has gotten into your bladder, you may expel urine inadvertently. There are some medications your doctor could prescribe, but my advice would be to cut down on all liquids after dinner, and work on urinating more than once before bedtime.

*Q. Why is the urge to "go" especially strong when I first get up in the morning?*

When you are asleep, you are asleep. What I mean by that very deep statement is that, although your bladder is filling up, you are not feeling an urge to pee. Also, you are lying flat, so the water is going to the back of the bladder. In the morning, when you stand up, the water drops by gravity to the valve area, and its sheer weight pushes to be released.

There is another time when urinary urgency hits—when you are uptight. Think about the last time you took an important exam or an experience of almost getting hit by a bus. A few seconds later, you just had to "go." Lots of adrenalin rushed into your system and increased your heart rate and thus your urine production.

*Q. Is it possible for the bladder to shrink, to get smaller?*

Yes. A chronically irritated bladder will respond by thickening its wall. Again, we are back to that balloon image. If the rubber gets thicker, the expandability of the balloon drops, and the amount of fluid that could be put into it decreases. As the balloon thickens, the *inside* area becomes smaller, and the need to go occurs more urgently.

We also know that some diabetics have problems with the nerve control of their bladders. And there are other nervous disorders (multiple sclerosis, Parkinson's disease, and spinal cord injuries) in which the muscles in the bladder wall are in constant semispasm. They are always semicontracted. This results in thickening of the bladder muscles, just the same as if you constantly exercised the biceps in your arm.

There is a surgical procedure to treat this condition, in which the surgeon selectively strips the nerves away from the bladder, not to make the bladder nonfunctional, but simply to get rid of those spasms and to get the bladder working more normally again.

*Q. When I get up to pee in the middle of the night, I seem to get a slight fever afterward. What might this be?*

Most of the time when you empty your full bladder abruptly, you get a realignment of your internal organs. And, by relieving pressure on the nerves that run over the sacral bone in the small of your back, you can get a fever type of response, or a strange sweating reaction. It is the same feeling as you might get after being hit by a low blow to your solar plexus. The fascinating name for this condition is *vasomotor instability*. Actually, the name is worse than the condition. Don't drink too much after dinner, urinate before going to bed, and forget about it.

*Q. Sometimes I have a burning sensation when I urinate. Can you suggest anything that would help?*

Cranberry juice. It is a urinary acidifier, and acid urine is normal healthy urine.

Alkaline or basic urine is often cloudy and will bring on that burning feeling because of an inflammation in your urinary tract. "Bad bugs" like this alkaline environment.

Get yourself some cranberry juice, and drink up to a quart a day. It acts as a urinary antiseptic. If you are worried about the calories, buy the artifically sweetened variety. If you don't like the taste, it mixes well with vodka for an evening aperitif.

As long as I'm on the subject of nutrition, I'd also advocate large doses of vitamin C to maintain an acid urine. I use two grams a day.

*Q. Once in a while, my urine smells just awful. My doctor told me not to worry, but when this happens at someone else's house it is most embarrassing.*

I agree with your doctor, not to worry. It may be food-related because as you are metabolizing certain foods in your body the waste products in your stool develop odors. The same holds true for your urine, especially after eating asparagus, which is a prime offender.

If you're not taking in enough fluids, your concentrated urine may have a stale odor. If by any chance you are taking large doses of vitamin B1, you may notice a urine and skin odor. (This is not completely bad, because at least it will keep the flies away from you.) Or, if there is some obstruction in the lower urinary tract, preventing a free flow, the urine can become brackish. It is like water trapped behind a dam. We have probably all experienced this condition; where our urine smells like ammonia.

When you do have this problem again, increase your fluid intake. And, if you keep track of the foods you have eaten prior to such a siege, you may find the exact dietary culprit and eliminate it.

*Q. I read that the prime minister of India, a man in his eighties, stays looking years younger by following a vegetarian diet. But he also has the rather unusual practice of drinking his own urine every morning, which he calls the staff of life. Could you comment?*

I find it difficult enough to face my cranberry juice in the morning. But to each his own.

When urine is not infected or has no odor, there is nothing wrong with it. People from some other civilizations believe that urine and feces are formed from one's own body forces and are not to be wasted. By consuming this waste matter, they feel they are recapturing their vital body energy. Actually, normal urine is sterile. But I do wonder if it isn't the prime minister's vegetarianism that is keeping him healthy, rather than his urine.

I remember comedian Alan King's story about the fellow in the hospital who had to give the nurse a urine specimen every day. Each time she said, "My, that's cloudy," or "My, that's clear." So one day, deciding to fool her, he poured apple juice into the specimen bottle. When she came in, he suddenly picked it up, drank it down, and commented, "OK, let's run that through again."

*Q. My husband was diagnosed as a diabetic six years ago, when he was thirty. Lately, I've noticed that when he urinates in the morning he starts, stops, starts, stops, like he's having to force it out. Is this something that should be checked?*

Absolutely. It could mean that he has some obstruction to the outlet of his urinary passageway. In a man of that age, one might find a fold in the lining membrane of his canal that could easily be stretched out. This is a simple office procedure.

Or it may be that he is losing some of the nerve senses of his bladder. Diabetics get some scarring of the blood vessels and nerve damage or neuritis. So the nerves that supply the bladder may not be working as well as they should. Therefore, when he tries to urinate he doesn't get quite enough push going in the first place, so he has to do multiple pushes. I certainly would have this checked at once by his urologist. Medications are available to stimulate bladder function.

*Q. If you use artificial sweeteners, do you stand a greater chance of getting cancer of the bladder?*

A federal ban was placed on such sweeteners recently, based on a Canadian study in which fifty-three men who had cancer of the bladder were also found to be users of artificial sweeteners.

Medical professionals believe that the Canadian study did *not* reach a valid conclusion. A human being would have to regularly drink eighty cans of diet drinks daily to provide enough artificial sweetener to approximate the bladder cancer test dose. Diabetics, who have no higher incidence of cancer of the bladder, do limit their sweetener intake to these artificial products.

*Q. Is there a relationship between smoking and cancer of the bladder?*

I'd be much more concerned about cigarettes than about saccharin. Males used to get bladder cancer at a six-to-one ratio over females, at the turn of the century. Now it is down to a three-to-one ratio, probably because women are smoking more.

There is absolutely *no question* that the incidence rate of bladder cancer is higher in smokers than in nonsmokers. In heavy smokers, a carcinogen (a cancer-causing agent) is absorbed into the lungs, filtered through the bloodstream, out through the kidneys, and into the bladder. We suspect that this carcinogen is probably a coal-tar derivative from the cigarette.

Curiously enough, smokers do not have a higher incidence of cancer of the kidney nor cancer of the ureter, the tube that carries the urine between the kidney and the bladder.

We do know that the bladder wall, which is made up of a different type of tissue, is definitely more highly susceptible to cancer. There is absolutely no question about it—this is a *dreadful* cancer, very hard to handle. And we really do not yet have any highly successful means of controlling it.

*Q. Are there danger signs to look for if you suspect cancer of the bladder?*

Blood in the urine is the single most important symptom in regard to the urinary tract. If there is blood in your urine, I would certainly advise you to see your physician *at once*, especially if there is *no pain* accompanying it.

Bladder cancer is tough enough at best. The earlier we find it, the better our chances are of getting a good cure. Unfortunately, in Senator Hubert Humphrey's case, the diagnosis was not made until many years after the initial problem started.

Often a person will discover blood in his or her urine, be horrified by it, and hope it will go away. That just doesn't happen. The onset of bleeding should be investigated immediately, because *fifty-eight percent* of all those who have painless, urinary bleeding *have a cancer somewhere in their urinary tract.* You can't afford to be an ostrich. Do not walk— *run* to your nearest doctor's immediately.

Physicians can do a Pap smear on urine, the same as a woman has done on her cervix. In over eighty percent of the cases, this initial study can show whether or not a tumor is present.

*Q. Does blood in your urine always mean you have bladder cancer?*

Far from it. I'm sorry if I gave you that impression. The most common reason you would have blood in your urine would be from an infection or inflammation of the bladder wall. Or you might have a stone in there, but usually you would experience a great deal of pain with the presence of a stone or infection.

*Q. What else could bring on bladder cancer?*

Where you *work* plays a big part. People exposed to pesticides have a far greater risk of bladder cancer. So do those who work in dry-cleaning establishments where napthalene is used. If you have a chronic irritation that keeps recurring, whatever the cause, cell changes can take place, leading to cancer.

*Q. Now that you've got me scared, how can I protect myself?*

Stop smoking. Get out of the agricultural fields and get somebody else to pick up your dry cleaning.

There are some theories regarding vitamins and their preventative effects on cancer of the bladder. Vitamin A, in daily dosages of 20,000 units, is reported to give a protective coating to the cells lining the urinary bladder. Dr. Linus Pauling believes that massive doses of vitamin C, at least twenty grams daily, keeps the cell wall intact, lessening the chances for the formation of a tumor. But don't start out on any large-scale vitamin program before first checking with your doctor regarding possible side effects.

*Q. How do you treat bladder cancer?*

The whole trick is early diagnosis. If your doctor can catch it quickly enough, he may be able to burn it out through a cystoscope. Or he may remove a pie-shaped wedge from the tumor-bearing bladder wall. Adequate tissue biopsy is imperative to determine tumor cell type as well as depth penetration into the bladder wall. In more advanced cases, heavy radiation may be indicated, followed by complete removal of the bladder.

There are other new diagnostic techniques available, one of which is a lymphangiogram. This outlines the glands around the bladder as to their involvement in the cancer. Computerized axial tomography (CAT scan) can give an electronic television readout on the extent of the tumor.

# Part Three

## *How It All Hangs Together— and Might Fall Apart*

THE INTEREST IN sex and in sexual dysfunction goes back to biblical times.

Remember the story where Adam is sitting on a rock in the Garden of Eden, and the Lord comes by and asks, "Adam, why are you sitting there looking so bored?"

And Adam says, "Well, Lord, I'm just bored. You know, we've looked at the flowers and we've picked the fruit. Isn't there something else we can do?"

And the Lord says, "Well, yes, you might try hugging Eve."

And Adam asks, "How do you do that?" So the Lord explains about hugging.

About ten days later, the Lord comes down the path, and there, again, is Adam, staring at a rock, bored. "What's the trouble, Adam, haven't you been hugging Eve?"

"Yes, Lord. But I'm sort of fed up with that. Isn't there something else we can do?"

"Well, you might try kissing Eve." And the Lord goes on to explain kissing.

At this point, Adam disappears for about three weeks. But, finally, once again, the Lord finds him staring at the same rock.

"Adam, haven't I given you lots of things to do? You mean you're bored again?"

"Lord, I've had it with this hugging and kissing. Isn't there something else we can do?"

"All right, Adam, why don't you go forth and multiply?" So, after explaining all about "multiplying," the Lord starts back down the path. After a few minutes, he hears footsteps behind him. And sure enough, there is Adam, racing after him.

"Lord, Lord. You've got to tell me one more thing. What's a 'headache'?"

Where did Adam go for advice? He had no one to turn to: no *Cosmopolitan*, no *Redbook*, no *Playboy*, no psychiatrist, no radio talk shows, and no group awareness sessions.

Today Adam could turn to a myriad of sources for help. But the answer is always within oneself. The average man has to realize that he's OK, sexually, and not feel he must measure up to the imaginary status of a Casanova, Romeo, James Bond, or Aly Khan. Don't make up problems that don't exist. There are enough that do. Good sex is good sex. Leave it alone.

*Q. We've been married eight years now and seem to be having sex less and less. We're down to once or twice a week. Are we normal?*

Perfectly. Maybe you would *like* more action, but, yes, you are normal. The *New England Journal of Medicine* (1978) reported a survey done among couples who admitted to having good marriages. The majority of them, who had been married from one to twenty years, said they had intercourse one to three times a week. Only 1 percent engaged in coitus every day, and 2 percent never had sex anymore. Interestingly enough, those who had sex the *least* ended up with the *most* male impotence and female frigidity.

*Q. How long do most men take in making love?*

The period of foreplay can be any length, whatever turns you on. But, after vaginal penetration, the average man will ejaculate within two minutes. He may remain erect for a while. The real test is whether he is able to satisfy his mate within that framework.

Have the answers to the last two questions sunk in yet? If the average couple makes love twice a week, averaging thirty minutes per encounter (foreplay and penetration), we're talking about 1 hour out of 168. Doesn't that make you wonder if sex within our culture is overemphasized?

*Q. Why does anyone today have any sexual problems? There are so many books on the market that tell you what to do—like, steps one through ten.*

One of the best-sellers in this field was *Joy of Sex* by Alex Comfort. If you haven't read it, you should, because it's really quite amusing. Comfort discusses the entire sex act as a *menu,* a gourmet guide to love-making. He starts with appetizers, goes on to the main course, and then to dessert. One of the major points is that the body, as a whole, is a sexual entity and that the skin is the best tactile organ we have. So sleeping in the buff, preferably in a double bed, can probably do a lot to revive a long-dormant sex life. Skin touching skin is, indeed, a fantastic turn-on. If I had my way, I'd do away with all king-sized beds. You certainly don't need a football field for this type of event.

One other point that Dr. Comfort makes is that every sex act need not be an Academy Award performance. The sex act should not be a wrestling match. You are making love, not war.

*Q. What do you think about these so-called sex therapists? You know—when a man is having trouble making love to his mate, he goes to one of these surrogate partners.*

I think I'll be more impressed the day when such a procedure is covered by Blue Cross. Of course, if that ever happens, sex surrogate therapy will be an exploding profession.

Seriously, there are some surrogates who are really very good at this sort of thing. One big problem is involvement with the client. Clients tend to imagine they are in love with the surrogate, and then they find it very difficult to disassociate themselves from that situation and from the situation at home that caused the problem in the first place. Often a man is very unhappy with his mate and is simply seeking a sexual adventure with a surrogate. He may very well go back to his wife no better off than he was to start with.

Under ideal circumstances, the role of the surrogate is to evaluate the love-making performance of the troubled male client. Comments and counseling are made along the way: before, during, and after the sex act.

Some men are thus reassured of their potency, while others are taught new techniques to please their mates and rearouse themselves.

*Q. What about sex counseling teams, where both the husband and wife get help from a member of their own sex?*

I much prefer this approach, where the counseling team does a joint physical examination with the other partner in the room. It's amazing how many men really don't know very much about their mate's anatomy, her erogenous zones, and so forth. And, equally, many women aren't that well informed about the male body.

Years ago, when the family physician was a close friend of the family, I would have preferred the medical approach. Today the qualified sex counseling team is probably the best approach. However, I would like to see state laws tightened to require that these people complete some courses of education that are acceptable to the Board of Medical Examiners, because there are a lot of quacks in this field.

I hear reports of some of these counselors punching their patients in the breast, pulling pubic hair, and having intercourse with them—"therapeutically," of course. I find this sort of thing totally unacceptable.

Some sex therapists I know are not sold at all on team counseling but use an individual approach, since often only one person in a couple is obviously in trouble.

*Q. What about the original Masters and Johnson approach of team counseling while spending two weeks in a hotel room?*

That was fine for those with the time and money to spare. But after the original two weeks you were sort of cast adrift. I prefer seeking help in your local community.

Most local health counseling now involves a more leisurely therapy: twelve to eighteen weeks. This way, you have the added advantage of having your therapists available at any time should another problem arise.

*Q. I have heard that a man is at the height of his sexual prowess while he's a teenager. True or false?*

Unfortunately, for us middle-aged types, true. A man's peak years as a sexual athlete are from seventeen to twenty-two. After that, it's all downhill—slowly, but definitely downhill. It recalls a phrase in an old song: "Why is youth wasted on the young?"

*Q. Wouldn't it hold true, then, that the perfect sexual mating would be a twenty-year-old man with a forty-year-old woman?*

Physically speaking, you are absolutely correct. The twenty-year-old man can produce more firm erections more often. But what about the *emotional* aspect? What would they talk about afterward? One cannot live by intercourse alone.

*Q. My husband, who is forty-five, has taken up sports and given up sex. He used to be a careful driver, and now he thinks he's racing at Indianapolis. Could this be because our kids are now off at college, and he's going through some male menopause thing?*

There is no real change in male hormone production until men are into their middle seventies. What we have here, the substitution of sport for sex, may be part of a psychological problem, which could also tie in with business pressures.

I also see here another very common problem—the reorientation of a marriage. Over the years, you have been occupied with the kids, not necessarily to the exclusion of your husband, perhaps. But you have had your priorities within the household, and he has had his at his work.

Now that the kids have left home, you are once again turning to him at a time when he feels he's really not needed that much around the house anymore. It isn't easy to get to know one another again, as when you were first married.

We call this the "empty nest" syndrome. Often, it is the woman who wants to get out of the house, to fling herself into various community activities. Here the situation is in reverse. He is now showing an indifference, or, at best, a casual interest in the day-to-day activities of your home life.

The problem can be turned around, and you may not like what I'm going to tell you, but it is now up to *you* to get *him* interested again.

*Q. Well, how do I do that? How do I become the young girl he married twenty-five years ago? We're not the same young kids. We've been through a lot together. A great deal of water has passed under the bridge.*

Just be more attentive to him. Give him some tender loving care. Hold his hand. Cook his favorite dinners.

You are not his mother. You are his wife and should never assume the mother role. You mentioned that you've been through a lot together. If you reflect on the *good* times and let your thoughts come through to him, there is no reason why that quarter-century bond can't be strengthened even further. You have so much that you have shared over the years as a basis for your romance. Develop new mutual activities. Stay in shape together, and above all communicate in a positive fashion.

*Q. I feel my husband has a deep-rooted psychological problem. He has pet names for our organs. He calls his penis "Charlie" and my vagina "Virginia."*

Many couples use pet names for their male and female organs. At its *best*, it can be used for a secret code. For example, a call to a man's office can relay the information that "Virginia wants to know if she can see Charlie tonight." Even without pet names, there are many people who just cannot bring themselves to use those good, old-fashioned, Anglo-Saxon four-letter words that seem to express things so well for the rest of us.

At its *worst*, it could indicate that your husband was overwhelmed by his parental conditioning. By naming his penis, he is copping out, distancing himself from sex. Charlie becomes a third person, so your husband is off the hook in what *he* believes is basically dirty and wrong.

*Q. I don't come to orgasm easily at all. My husband really has to stimulate my clitoris a lot. Do I have something wrong with me, physically or psychologically?*

There would be a physical problem if your clitoris is covered by a skin hood and not easily exposed to stimulation. But some women are just slower than others.

All orgasm in the female begins in the clitoris, not within the vaginal canal. That's why the size of a man's penis has no bearing on his ability to give a woman sexual satisfaction. Just as long as he's got an organ (even if it's only moderately erect) and can rub it across the clitoris, after a woman has had adequate foreplay, it will excite her and lead to orgasm.

*Q. But I seem to have to be stimulated at the same time we're having intercourse, which is putting my husband in an impossible situation.*

Not really. I'd suggest you experiment with changing positions a little. Have your husband enter you, higher, more over your abdomen so that his penis makes better contact with your clitoris at the time of insertion and withdrawal.

*Q. My husband and I haven't had sex in over three years. He's on the road for weeks at a time in his business. When he does come home, he shows no interest in sex at all. Yet he claims he is not playing around when he's away. Am I being too naive in believing him?*

Something or someone is turning him off. Maybe it's his job. Maybe it's within himself. Or maybe it's you!

*Q. I forgot to mention that he collects pornography. He has stacks of those books and magazines.*

Then I cannot believe he is not interested in sex. He is either finding his action on the road, or he is masturbating.

*Q. We all know that a woman is capable of multiple orgasms. I just read about multiple male orgasms. If such a thing is possible, I want to get my share.*

If anybody had asked me this ten years ago, I would have enjoyed a quiet snicker.

But now there is a new concept based on the belief that ejaculation and orgasm are *not* the same thing. Ejaculation involves the actual release of the fluid from the penis, while what you are *feeling* is the orgasm, the climactic sensation.

Multiple male orgasms lead a man into a series of sexual peaks and valleys. He is stimulated to a peak of *feeling*, where his body shows all the signs of orgasm: heavy breathing, increased heart rate, light sweating, testes elevation, and muscle contractions. Then, prior to actual ejaculation, he retreats to a tranquil valley by self-conditioning, which may involve some mental gymnastics. When he's in control of his body again, he ascends to a new peak and then again turns off.

Not every man can do this. Not every man would *want* to do this.

*Q. My girl simply cannot achieve orgasm by normal intercourse. What happens is this: After I've withdrawn, she takes my penis and works it against her clitoris. That's the only way she can be satisfied, but it sure is painful to me. Her doctor told her that her clitoris was covered by an extra skin thickness and that this could be corrected surgically. Is this a difficult operation?*

Her doctor is referring, actually, to a female circumcision. What's happening is that she's getting some thickness around the clitoris so that it can't be adequately retracted. Normally, if you pull up just below the pubic area in a woman, just above the vagina, you'll notice that the clitoris exposes itself.

In some women, however, the clitoris is bound down by little adhesions or scar tissue, or by the vaginal lips overhanging the area. By trimming away some of this excess tissue, and exposing the clitoris it becomes more sensitive.

To answer your question, this is not a major operation. It's a simple surgical correction, and it should free her entire clitoris to sensitivity—not just the tip or a side.

*Q. For years, we American men have taken the brunt of being called lousy lovers. Isn't there a new survey that shows that we are just as disappointed in American women?*

That's true. In *Beyond the Male Myth*, Dr. Anthony Pietropinto and Jacqueline Simenauer (1977) state that the major irritant to men is when their women seem cold or disinterested. In reply to the question, "What would you like to do most often," the top male choices were (1) "try different sexual positions" and (2) "engage in more oral sex," which the authors have termed the "fastest growing turn-on in America."

Overwhelmingly, the men surveyed wanted their women to be more aggressive and to take a more active sex role. They also wanted them to be loving and considerate. They wonder what happened to the sexually "turned-on" woman they knew at the beginning of their relationship who became less interested later on, as other factors intruded, such as career and family.

We men are conditioned in our love making by a confusing mixture of Victorian culture and advanced sexual attitudes. We are not born great lovers—we need all the help we can get.

*Q. All right, I'm willing to go along with this and try new things with my husband, but you just can't dictate instant feelings and shout out "position number 17." Instant intimacy is impossible.*

I agree. Intimacy can often begin at the breakfast table, before going to work. A touch, a smile, a caress, an attempt at being attractive over bacon and eggs can implant the notion in both of you that tonight is going to be a very special time.

When you both get home, there are other little signals of arousal: for her, perhaps additional perfume and fluffing of the hair; for him, a fresh shave; and a shower together, a little better-than-usual dinner and an extra hug. These are the signals that mean tonight's the night. The way has been paved for an amorous evening. Now is the time to communicate, to say "I like it better upsidedown," or to slowly work your way into position 17.

What a difference between what I've just described and "You think *you've* had a lousy day? Let me tell you about *mine.*"

*Q. Doctor, I don't know if this is in your field or not, but I often have sexual dreams. And my partner isn't my husband.*

That's quite common. You are a normal woman.

*Q. But when I am having these dreams I can have an actual orgasm without any stimulation.*

Again, you're normal. In fact, many people probably wish they could be as normal as you. Dreams and fantasy play a large part in our sex lives. Many couples sustain their marriages largely by virtue of the fact that they can fantasize a different partner. This may not be the happiest of situations, but it certainly does exist. I do not, however, look forward to the day when couples will go to a store, buy Farrah Fawcett and Lee Majors masks, and really put this fantasy trip to the ultimate test.

*Q. Do both men and women enjoy the same sexual fantasies and get turned on by pornography?*

Indeed they do. Tests have been conducted showing that both sexes get aroused by porno books or films. These experiments measured the male's erection and the amount of vaginal lubrication secreted by the female.

A generation ago, most women didn't know what pornographic films *were,* although they heard rumors about stag movies being shown at mens' smokers. But today many women who would not be caught dead in a hard-core porno theatre or adult book shop are almost demanding to see 'Deep Throat" in their homes or with a small gathering of friends. And now that home video recorders are available, pirated editions of pornographic films are rampant on the marketplace, in cassette form. Pornography *is* a mutual turn-on.

*Q. Do some men have to have sex daily?*

Yes, some men do—and sometimes more than once. Often they have feelings of insecurity, which are manifested by hostility toward women. These men are indiscriminate in their sexual contacts—whomever, whenever, wherever—simply bodies that touch in passing. They are incapable of maintaining a sustained relationship and must constantly re-prove their manhood to themselves.

*Q. Every time I make love to my wife, I get what you might call blisters on my penis. This causes me a great deal of discomfort. It also takes about a week to heal before any other activity can take place. Is this my problem or my wife's?*

I'd say it is a mutual problem, wouldn't you? Since you don't have these irritation sites at times other than intercourse, I would presume that your wife could be transmitting something to you. Now, this may not be a venereal disease. It may be a chemical reaction. It may be a change in the character of her vaginal secretions. Many men report burning on their skin after intercourse.

I suggest two courses of action, and I advise you to follow them both.

First, after making love, don't spend a long time in bed. I don't mean "sprint," but get up fairly soon and wash yourself off thoroughly. Soap and rinse yourself. Then apply powder—common ordinary baby powder. Powder tends to absorb any liquid material that may still be present. It will act as a lubricant for the skin and will protect it later.

Secondly, ask your wife to make an appointment immediately with her gynecologist for a vaginal examination. She may have something going on in her that needs to be looked at, perhaps some acidic or fungal condition that is inadvertently being transferred to you.

*Q. I have the reverse problem. I have a lot of burning inside me when my husband ejaculates. Why?*

This is caused by a vaginal irritation or infection and is, essentially, your problem. Prompt diagnosis and treatment by your doctor will relieve this situation immediately. Marriage can be irritating in more ways than one.

*Q. I'll testify to that irritation. My husband is in the military, and when he does get home and we have sex, I get a terrible bladder infection every time. Is there any medication that can clear it up?*

Your problem is actually quite common with women who have no sex for a while and then bursts of activity all at once. We call this condition "honeymoon cystitis." Check with your doctor. He will determine whether this represents inflammation or true infection.

Your vagina can be a reservoir of potential problems. Every time you have sex, your own vaginal fluid may be pushed into your bladder, causing this irritation. Medications are available to relieve this situation and should be started several days before your husband gets home.

Something else you might try is drinking a glass of water before and after sex to increase urination and flush out the bladder and urinary passage.

*Q. I know I'm not the young buck anymore, what with the sagging belly and the whole bit. I've been reading lately that all this fat can be cut away by plastic surgery. How do you feel about this?*

Unenthusiastic. Look, how many of us could really qualify for the centerfold of "Playgirl?" Many of us have sagging tummies and lumps and bumps. I believe that if the *sight* of a female or male body is not a turn-on, certainly *touching* is, which brings us right back to that old double bed and sleeping in the buff.

I cannot endorse this type of body surgery, which, believe me, is a major operative procedure, fraught with complications, especially increased chances of infection. Fatty tissue does not heal well. The scars you are left with may be more unsightly than the fat you just got rid of. Try some abdominal exercises on a regular basis. They will work wonders.

And so will a diet. I just heard of a new one that doesn't involve hard-boiled eggs, grapefruit, or chicken legs. You can eat what you want, *but* you must eat with four naked fat people.

*Q. My gynecologist has prescribed a vaginal cream that has hormones in it. I'm concerned that if any of this gets on my husband's penis, it might be absorbed into his system.*

Don't worry. Remember that your vaginal lining is the same kind of mucous membrane that lines your mouth, eyes, rectum, and nose. And that's the kind of membrane that you absorb from very quickly.

The penis has skin on it, and true skin does not absorb that hormone in much of a quantity. If your husband did absorb any, it would be so infinitesmal there would be no effect on him at all. If anything, it should improve your love life, by making your vagina moister and more receptive to his entering.

*Q. Doctor, I seem to perform at my very best when there is some danger involved, like being discovered or walked in on.*

In the "Pink Panther" movies, the intrepid Inspector Clouseau tells his Japanese houseboy, Cato, to attack him "any time." Some men *do* get turned on by danger.

Others say that spontaneous sex is the best, and many of my younger associates describe how great it is on the coffee table, on the floor, wherever it occurs. I keep thinking—Good Lord, how uncomfortable!

Actually, many folks in their twenties have the philosophy that sex must be spontaneous—when the spirit moves them. It may move them on a staircase or on an outdoor swing. The most common fantasy is that you are making love to someone other than your regular partner at the time. Don't feel particularly guilty about this, either, because your partner may be playing the identical game.

Fantasy can play a most important part in your sex life. Fantasy can make a turn-off into a turn-on. Fantasy is normal.

*Q. Let me ask you about a real danger. What do you do when your six-year-old walks in while you're having sex?*

This is not only a real danger but also a very common one that has probably happened to many of us at one time or another. I can't give you the definitive answer, and neither can anyone else.

I asked a number of my colleagues how they would handle it, and I received answers that ranged from "I threw a book at him" to "I kindly asked him to please go out and close the door." It's best not to make a big thing of it. Owen posed this question to his nine-year-old step-daughter, Ashley. Her reply was "You mean if I'd come in when—oh, gross, the whole thing is gross. I'd get out of there as fast as I could." Again, that reflects the latent period in a child's life between five and prepuberty.

A radio listener told me this recently happened to her husband and herself, when their eight-year-old burst in on a Sunday morning with something he wanted to show them. "Whoops," he said, "Sorry," and went back downstairs. Since it sort of destroyed their moment of ecstasy, they went down to talk to their son to find out if he knew what was going on.

"It looked like you and Dad were making a baby."

The mother replied, "No, Daddy had a vasectomy, so you and your sister are the only two children we'll have."

"You mean it was just fun and games?"

"That's right."

"Well, that's fine. Two kids are enough around here anyway. Just so it was fun and games."

*Q. I'm a professional boxing fan, and for years I've heard conflicting stories about sports and sex. Should an athlete abstain from sex prior to an important athletic event?*

I don't think it really makes any difference one way or another. Oh, sure, I've read that an athlete may abstain from sex for weeks before competition. A training camp may be set up out in the woods, away from all sexual temptations.

Yet I also hear about the sexual freedom in Olympic Villages, involving young men and women from nations around the world. These athletes claim they *need* to release their tension sexually. They're in perfect shape. Everything is flowing in their bodies: good blood circulation, good lymph circulation, proper diet. They are in top condition and, of course, they are sexually stimulated. I really don't believe that normal intercourse is going to deprive them of any bodily function.

*Q. My wife hasn't been feeling well for the past six months or so, and I've been masturbating more and more. Yet I feel guilty about it.*

Join the club, the members of which still regard masturbation as something dirty. It's a very big club. Starting with puberty, 92 percent of all men masturbate during their life. And, surprisingly enough, 58 percent of all women. Women of all ages are, in fact, still discovering this outlet.

But, getting back to your problem. Again, use it or lose it. Masturbation is a release of tension. Most importantly, it keeps that old transportation system going from the testes to the prostate to the ejaculate. Interestingly enough, a number of men who were separated from their wives for long periods of time, such as military service overseas, came home and never got interested in sex again because they didn't "use it."

There is another factor that affects who masturbates and why. For men, there is a definite correlation between education and masturbation. The better educated you are, the more likely you are to choose this as a sexual release. Perhaps, the higher degree of education a man has, the less fearful he is of masturbation as a health hazard. With women, however, there is no connection between the two.

As far as the unmarrieds and marrieds go, the frequency of masturbation averages out at twice a week for the first group and once a month for the latter. Of course, the more sexually active the couple, the less frequent the masturbation.

*Q. I am a businessman, on the road a lot. And I find a correlation between how good sales are and how much I masturbate.*

That's not unusual. Overachievers seem to be overmasturbators. When things go well, these men want it to go even better. Also, the more ingenious the man, the more apt he is to seek out additional mechanical aids to further enhance his solo performance. I have heard of men who plug in a vacuum cleaner and envision its sucking action as the equivalent of oral copulation (Shanor, 1978).

*Q. I masturbate a lot. Can this affect my normal sex relations?*

Masturbation is a lonely act and is not associated with interpersonal feelings. A man's sexual partner may not be available at particular times. Therefore, when he does masturbate during those periods, he is unwarrantedly ashamed of the act and is fearful of being caught.

To answer your question—*yes*, it can affect normal sex relations. Another problem with masturbation in a man who is still sexually active is that it tends to shorten the regular sex act. When these men do have relationships, they are prone to premature ejaculations. Most men who masturbate do not do it for prolonged episodes but simply for a quick release of tension. This "let's get it over with" approach may still be in the back of their minds when they make love to a woman. Unhappily, there are a lot of women, who, because of their disinterest in sex, are perfectly content that their mates are masturbating and leaving them alone.

*Q. I've heard that one of the dangers of masturbation is that it shortens a man's sex life.*

That's an interesting observation. It's completely *untrue*, of course, but interesting. This is based on the old "voo-doo" idea that each man has a limited number of ejaculations during his lifetime, as if when he's born he's given a ration book, with $x$ number of ejaculations in it. So each act of masturbation takes away one chance at sex. Actually, the *reverse* is true. The more active you *are*, sexually, the more active you will continue to be.

# Stress, Exercise, Nutrition — It All Adds Up to Sex

Let's say you were born with the right number of organs in the proper places and that they all seem to be working. Does that automatically give you a 50,000-mile or fifty-year guarantee (whichever comes first) that your sex life is going to be terrific? Hardly. What about *your* fuel, maintenance, road conditions, and upkeep? In body language, that means your nutrition habits, your exercise schedule, and how you handle stress.

Have you ever noticed that, during your annual two-week vacation, all of your sexual problems seem to disappear? You feel better. You are more relaxed. You and your mate seem to be with it again, any time, any place. Unfortunately, vacations do come to an end and you have to face up to those *other fifty* weeks. For many men, that means back to the battlefield of life.

Surveys have shown that 90 percent of us are not that overjoyed with what we do for a living. So what are your options? Gripe about it and continue to live with stress? Change jobs to a field you think you will enjoy? Go into business for yourself? Or continue to do what you are doing now, only with a new philosophy? By that, I mean, you can still do your job well but you don't have to take it so seriously. Start thinking a little more along the lines of "Take the Money and Run." Use those dollars for *your* own benefit. Instead of two weeks once a year, start spreading things out. Plan long weekends. Get away more often.

The military has known about this forever. A man on the front lines has an increased adrenalin flow and a decreased male hormone level. His suppressed sex drive can spring back astonishingly quickly with some "R and R."

Rest and relaxation mean different things to different individuals. One man may want to test his physical strength by climbing a mountain. Another may get his enjoyment reading a spy novel in his backyard hammock. There is no one-two-three magic formula for how to relax.

But you had better start thinking about which is more important to you: a telephone in your car or a satisfying sex life? Stress builds up in your mind and in your body. I can't get into your mind. That's your job. But I can suggest that you had better start using that body of yours, and I don't mean sitting at a desk.

The one comment I will *not* accept from you is, "But, Doctor, I don't have *time* to jog, to sail, to take up a hobby." Each new morning hands you twenty-four fresh hours. You *work* about eight and *sleep* about eight, right? Now you tell *me* what's left—*time* is left. *Use it.*

*Q. Exercise, you say? I haven't gained any weight in years. Why do I need things like jogging?*

You don't, other than to keep your heart and lungs in shape. Jogging won't do much for your penis, I'll admit, but staying alive *is* fairly important.

Personally, jogging bores the hell out of me. Before every runner in the world hangs me in effigy, let me say that I *do* feel it is a fine body conditioner because of its consistency, much better than a sudden stop-start sport like racquetball.

For those who want to *start* an exercise program, especially senior citizens, T. P. & W.—"take-pains-and-walk." The whole concept of exercise is to gently stimulate your heart and to expand your lungs by breathing more deeply. You don't necessarily have to be bathed in sweat to accomplish these ends. To achieve maximum benefit, you should walk briskly and steadily, starting with ten minutes a day and working yourself up to several hours a week.

In modern society, where can you best walk without getting mugged? You certainly don't want to frequent a poorly lighted neighborhood at night. Why not a couple of turns around and through your well-illuminated local shopping center, where you can people-watch and windowshop at the same time?

*Q. Thanks a lot! I've just taken up racquetball. I have heard it's the best exercise you can get in a limited amount of time.*

Did I hear that word *time* again?

I actually have no complaints about racquetball for young studs, although they are the ones who need body toning the least. However, for anyone over forty, I'd suggest a stress EKG test (treadmill) before even considering it.

The best supersex exercises don't require any special equipment like running shoes, warmup suits, or paddles.

*Q. What are these supersex exercises that will help me in the sack?*

If heavy breathing and lots of sweat turn you on, then start turning the pedals of a *bicycle.* I don't care if it is outdoors and you are running into the backsides of joggers or if you are perched on a stationary bike at home watching "Charlie's Angels." The important thing here is the *pumping action*, which pushes blood around the lower portion of your body, especially through your prostate and your penis.

Swimming would be my alternative choice, but, I mean, *really* swimming, not dog paddling. Start slowly and work up to twenty laps a day, or more.

*Q. Lately, right in the middle of making love, I've been getting muscle spasms. It really turns me and my partner off, fast.*

That doesn't surprise me. If a man suddenly has to jump out of bed just when things get going good, that certainly can lead to a limp penis and a frustrated partner. I'm sure your mate wants a lover, not a leaper. The secret here is keeping yourself *limber.*

A baseball player takes batting and fielding practice right before the game to limber up. I'm not suggesting you shag flies before hopping in the sack. But a trip to a disco a couple of hours earlier will help limber up the muscles of your abdomen, hips, and back. If you're not near a disco, or if the music has ended and the malady lingers on, try duck waddling: You turn your feet outward and walk like Charlie Chaplin while squatting slightly.

Here are three more exercises. First, kneel with one knee on the floor and your other leg straight out in front. Bend your body forward as far as possible, then back as far as possible. Alternate to the other knee. Second, assume the position of a football lineman in the three-point stance, putting one foot well in front of the other. Then lunge forward slightly. Third, you might even try doing a gentle straddle over the corner of your bed to stretch and tone your thigh muscles.

*Q. Are there any exercises that can directly help make me a better lover?*

There certainly are. And I'll throw in two more benefits—stamina and power.

For example, did you know that your penis has muscles? These are the same set of muscles that enable you to start and stop your urine flow. They also play a part in your erections. As you are reading this, try tightening the area between your testicles and your rectum. Tighten, loosen. Repeat again and again. You should feel your penis twitch.

Now that I've gotten you in the mood, here is another. Pull in your belly muscles below the navel, tighten your rectum, and try to pull your penis up. You must breath above the navel, while pulling in below. This exercise is a bit reminiscent of the *bump* portion of burlesque's bump-and-grind routines. Don't be a belly breather.

Either of these exercises can be done any time, anywhere: standing up, sitting down, at work, at home, in your car.

*Q. Earlier, you mentioned food and sex. I don't see what one has to do with the other.*

Try telling that to Adam. Didn't an apple start the whole thing? Food and sex have gone hand in hand ever since the Garden of Eden.

You can tell a lot about a person's sex life by the way he or she eats. A man who enjoys food is more likely to enjoy other sensual experiences, including sex. By enjoy, I mean the man who savors the aroma, who appreciates the presentation, who looks forward to dining, rather than standing at a lunch counter, gulping down plastic fast food.

I am not talking about the man who stuffs himself. As with anything else, there is a point of diminishing utility. An *over*eater is an *under*-performer. The blood that he needs for his erection is diverted from his penis to his gut, while the excess calories are well on their way to his oversized belly. Remember that the shortest distance between two bodies is not around a fat gut.

*Q. I'll buy your thoughts on the enjoyment of food, short of stuffing ourselves. But does it make any difference what we eat?*

Protein is the main support of the body, while carbohydrates and fats simply add calories. If you are thinking, "Hell, I can burn off calories fast enough with sexual activity," think again. Sex only burns off 100 calories with your everyday-type partner; but that's it—100 calories, period. If you are into orgies, with a variety of partners, who knows? That might even surpass racquetball.

No matter how intense your sexual activity, protein is still the main support of the body. To get that protein, you don't have to borrow on next week's salary to buy a supply of steaks and prime ribs. Try vegetable proteins, such as soybeans, lima beans, and peas. Fish is not only high in protein and low in fat, but it's also a symbol of potency. How many thousands of eggs *does* the average male salmon fertilize?

Speaking of eggs, they offer you two distinct benefits. Not only are they high in protein, but they are also a prime source of cholesterol, which is the base of our sex hormones. Many men feel the *raw* egg carries the sexual connotation of the beginning of life. People have put raw eggs in their milkshake, juice, or beer for years.

So much for the good news. Now for the bad: I want you to *give up* all saturated fats and fried foods and don't be a "junk food junkie."

*Q. How do you feel about vitamins and minerals? I keep hearing that zinc is the new "in" thing.*

Reportedly, without *zinc,* there is no *zest.* Zinc is a must for a healthy prostate gland and in the production of testosterone. When you ejaculate, the zinc present in your fluid should be replaced. How?

You don't have to run to your health food store for a huge bottle of zinc if you eat plenty of pumpkin seeds, rabbit, onions, nuts, liver, gelatin, whole wheat bread, and shellfish. This explains the historical aphrodisiac effect attributed to oysters. Alcohol, incidentally, washes the zinc out of your system. So if you drink and *don't* eat any of the aforementioned foods, maybe you *should* jog to your health food store.

*Q. What else might help? I keep hearing about the B vitamins and brewer's yeast.*

So do I, yet nobody has the definitive answer, not only on vitamin B and brewer's yeast, but also in regard to the three trace minerals magnesium, manganese, and iron. If you are truly deficient in these substances, you'll probably feel better if you replace them. If you are not deficient, they are not going to do you any harm.

B vitamins and brewer's yeast are reported to influence the production of the male sex hormone and may increase your performance in the bedroom. Originally, brewer's yeast was considered to be of nutritional value because it contained large amounts of protein. The newest thinking is that brewer's yeast also contains large amounts of selenium, the least abundant of the essential minerals. There is also talk today about potassium aiding in stress and fatigue situations. Many airline travelers are taking it to cut down on jet lag.

We can talk all we want to about vitamins A through Z and minerals from aluminum to zinc. But, as far as sex is concerned, *love is the most important dietary supplement.*

*Q. Every time I ask my doctor about vitamins and dietary supplements, he gives me a blank stare. I gather he doesn't believe in them.*

Or he doesn't know anything about them. Nutrition has never been a major subject in medical school, if, indeed, it was covered at all. Today, you can listen to all the "pro" and "con" vitamin arguments and still be confused. The facts are not all in.

Biochemist Dr. Richard Passwater (1977) contends that vitamin E does prevent and cure heart disease, is an anticlotting agent, and increases the blood's supply of oxygen.

Vitamin C is supposed to prevent heart disease and protect you from the common cold. Some scientists now claim that mega doses of vitamin C can prevent or cure cancers. Another school of thought says that if you are a heavy smoker you should be taking, at least, ten grams of vitamin C daily to replenish the loss in your body.

Nutrition is a big subject in itself. Check your public library or bookstore. You'll find reams of material available on vitamins, minerals, and food additives.

I, personally, believe in vitamin supplements. While I can't prove that I am right, you can't prove that I am wrong.

# Sexually Transmitted Disease (S.T.D.)

You may be delighted to know that the world of medicine now has a brand new name for what were once called venereal diseases.

Of course, a change in nomenclature will not make you feel any better if you've noticed symptoms of sores, chancres, discharges or burning urination. The new terminology is "S.T.D."—sexually transmitted diseases. Actually, some of these microbes can be picked up without intercourse at all. Yes, Virginia, there really *are* toilet-seat "bugs"—lesser-known but highly contagious ailments such as herpes and NGU.

Among the gifts that Columbus received when he discovered America was syphilis, the result of sexual intercourse with infected native Americans. This disease, which was then unknown in Europe, became the genital scourge of the Middle Ages. Currently it has dropped to fourth place in our S.T.D. list, mostly because penicillin has been so effective against it. In fact, anyone who has been hospitalized for anything over the past two decades has been automatically checked for syphilis. Let's face it, syphilis scares people. They become much more concerned and more apt to seek immediate medical treatment than if they had contracted gonorrhea, for example. But, they should realize that gonorrhea has its own disastrous ramifactions.

Actually, when you are talking about S.T.D., most of the time you are referring to gonorrhea. Except for the common cold, gonorrhea is the most contagious communicable disease in the country today.

Gonorrhea is particularly prevalent among our younger population, as they are experimenting sexually at a younger age and with more partners. Youths fifteen to nineteen, who constitute less than 10 percent of our citizenry, account for 22 percent of all reported cases of gonorrhea. Expand the demographics to include the fifteen- to thirty-five-year-old group, and you will account for 90 percent of gonorrhea today.

I find it incredible and irresponsible that so many men will not seek medical aid if they feel they have picked up a dose! If he doesn't care about the physical harm that will come to him, what about the physical effects on his mate, and babies they may want to bring into this world? For gonorrhea, together with syphilis, herpes, and a whole slew of S.T.D.'s are frequently transmitted to the newborn.

Sure, in the old days, gonorrhea meant a heap of trouble for the patient. In my training years, which was just about the time penicillin was introduced, there was no real treatment for gonorrhea. One school of thought was to inject the patient with a typhoid vaccine or malaria. This would create a very high body temperature and, theoretically, kill the organisms.

If left untreated the consequences of gonorrheal infection were potentially very harmful. The man's urinary passageway might become very irritated, possibly forming scar tissue and narrowing down. This condition is called a stricture. Our father's and grandfather's urinary canals would then have to be stretched at a doctor's office indefinitely. The doctor used long graduated metal instruments called sounds, a far cry from today's antibiotics. A temporarily sore rear end from today's injections is paradise compared to the not so olden days. Yet the patient must seek help. Men know something is wrong, whereas at least 80 percent of women do not have any apparent symptoms in the early stages of S.T.D. So, you see, it has to be the man who admits he is in trouble.

Here is something else to remember with regard to both syphilis and gonorrhea. You cannot protect yourself ahead of time with a preventive vaccine for either disease. A condom might offer some protection but not if oral-genital sex is the game of the day. For women, the birth control pill offers absolutely no barrier against a sexually transmitted disease. Anyone who thinks it does better enroll in Sex Education I.

The tragic aspect to this is that of all people who contract gonorrhea or syphilis, 20 percent will become reinfected and have to seek treatment again. THERE IS NO IMMUNITY AGAINST RE-INFECTION.

Why the increase in this easily treated problem? In many cases, casual sex means anonymous sex—partners don't even know each other's last names. Under these circumstances, public health officials find themselves at a dead end trying to trace down all these contacts.

In addition, physicians often have difficulty communicating with their patients about S.T.D. Doctors are embarrassed to ask their patients not only about the number, but also the gender of their consorts. S.T.D. involves at least two people, and any person who has a diagnosed infection should assume the responsibility of informing his contacts. Rarely do people do so.

*Q. My husband got syphilis two years ago. He did go to the doctor's and was treated with penicillin. But I am still afraid of having sex with him, even after all this time. Can the disease recur?*

Not likely. If it was treated adequately, it is probably cured. A blood test might diagnose his present condition and put your mind at rest. The problem is that once a person has had syphilis, even though he has taken heavy amounts of antibiotics (especially penicillin), a positive blood test reaction can exist without the active disease itself.

The signs of primary-degree syphilis are usually chancre sores on the body that do not heal without treatment. In more advanced cases, neurological changes occur, such as shuffling gait, inability to raise the feet, and loss of memory. Joint changes, particularly in the knees, may be experienced. Other bones, such as the nose, may eventually rot away.

If he doesn't have those difficulties, I'd say he is safe. With an adequate course of antibiotics, the chances of recurrence are extremely remote.

There may be a psychological problem within yourself. It could be that your husband's *affair* is bothering you more than the disease that is now cured.

*Q. I think I've got gonorrhea, and I've got to admit I have been too scared to do anything about it. Am I asking for trouble?*

You just answered your own question. YES!

For one thing, the glands within your urinary passageway will tend to swell and scar, eventually leading to a restriction of the urinary flow. This is the "stricture" I described previously. This scarring may also close the sperm ducts and leave you sterile.

If left unchecked, these germs tend to spread to the bloodstream, resulting in gonorrheal ulcers of the eye and, even more commonly, in gonorrheal arthritis. This is a dreadful arthritis, because you can end up with a fused or nonfunctioning joint. Untreated gonorrhea can also result in disease of the heart valves and even meningitis.

*Q. How long could one walk around with gonorrhea before these negative effects set in?*

You might have six months' grace. But remember, if you wait that long to get medical aid and if the arthritis is already underway, you're in big trouble. We can prevent the condition from becoming more progressive, but we cannot undo the damage that has already occurred.

*Q. That may be what I had. After I contracted a venereal disease, my doctor diagnosed it as gonococcal arthritis. I got a penicillin shot, and I thought it went away. But two weeks later it showed up in my bloodstream and attacked all my joints. Then I received more massive doses of penicillin. Even today, my joints ache once in a while.*

When a patient complains of arthritis, they have certain characteristic changes in the joints, which are visible by X ray. On tapping the joint fluid, you can recover the infecting organism by stain or culture. This means treating vigorously with penicillin combined with a blocking agent called *probenecid*. It prevents the kidneys from excreting the penicillin and keeps the body levels of the drug very high, the better to clout the organism with.

One major problem is, once you have arthritis (with its inflammation of the joints), whatever the cause, it tends to recur even though the precipitating factors have gone.

*Q. Is this the supergonorrhea that is coming in from the Far East?*

It is Far Eastern in origin, usually brought in by servicemen, from Japan, Hong Kong, Vietnam, or the Philippines. This gonococcus is all the same strain. And the adjective *super* describes problems we have in fighting it.

Recently, the Center for Disease Control (CDC) in Atlanta has recommended that double or triple the usual dose of penicillin be the drug of choice. Interestingly enough, the new CDC recommendations for gonorrhea now are 4.8 million units of Penicillin G. We used to think that 1.2 million units would do the job. Since a cc is roughly 30 drops, and each cc contains only 600,000 units, with the new recommendations, we're now talking about an injection of some 240 drops into your rump. Believe me, it hurts us as much to give that injection, since we know what the patient is going to experience when he tries to sit down.

Penicillin is still our first line of defense, but, unhappily, many people are allergic to it. We have found out, however, that this Vietnamese strain is often resistant to all levels of penicillin. There is a new drug called Spectinomycin, which is supposedly specifically formulated for this disease. However, this is usually considered to be about the fourth line of defense. Unfortunately, the organism builds up a resistance very early to this particular medication. We would first try many of the tetracyclines and other medications prior to using Spectinomycin.

*Q. But what's the difference, basically, between the new supergonorrhea and regular gonorrhea?*

With the supergonorrhea, the individual usually experiences a more profuse urethral discharge and more severe pain. The CDC's recommended penicillin dosage schedule is ineffective, as are many of the other commonly used antibiotics. The medications that are most effective, unfortunately, have very serious side effects themselves, such as prolonged intestinal inflammation. So we do not like to prescribe these drugs lightly or for long periods of time.

With regard to the continued spread of this superstrain, we are running into another problem. How do you trace the contacts of a germ that may have originated in Vietnam, for example?

*Q. What are the symptoms of the two strains? Do they differ at all?*

They may not. They both involve a urethral discharge and a burning sensation during urination. The only real difference is in their immediate response (or lack of response) to therapy.

*Q. Would you say that gonorrhea has reached epidemic proportions?*

Let's not use the word *epidemic* too freely. First, consider another word—*endemic.* This means there is a constant disease reservoir always present, but it does not reach what we consider to be above normal levels. When it does rise above these levels, then we consider it to be epidemic.

Nationwide, gonorrhea is probably endemic. In major seaport cities, with their profusion of prostitutes and servicemen bringing in different bacterial strains from other lands, it is probably epidemic.

*Q. Let's say I had gonorrhea years ago and never did anything about it. But after that I was given antibiotics for some other problem. Could that have cured my original infection?*

Very easily. Subsequent doses of antibiotic medication, say for an abscessed tooth or sinus infection, could quite effectively have cured the primary infection.

I should point out that quite a few cases of gonorrhea subside by themselves. They may be self-limited by natural body defenses, so-called host resistance. They may not be gone but just dormant, and any drop in body defenses might increase the chance of reactivating the disease. Secondary disease effects, like gonorrheal arthritis, cause permanent changes and do not revert to normal, even after subsequent antibiotic treatment.

*Q. Are there people walking around who may have gonorrhea and not know it?*

Yes, especially women. Sometimes the early symptoms are very mild: often a slight burning urination. Some individuals just don't pay attention to these signs, or they may be ignorant of the fact that this disease could occur in them. There are an awful lot of women who find themselves pregnant and still say, "It can't happen to me!"

This lack of symptoms may also be seen in some men but more frequently in women. In men, there is usually a yellowish discharge from the penis that starts about three days after sexual contact.

*Q. Why would someone try to hide a venereal disease?*

Let's say a fellow is married and picked up gonorrhea on the outside. Now he has the additional problem of possibly having infected his wife, too. He knows we have to make a report to the county health officer with his given name and address. However, because of today's laws we cannot invade his right of privacy.

So if a patient comes to a urologist and says "I have a discharge," we can *ask* him for his name and address, but legally he doesn't have to provide any I.D., such as a Social Security card or a driver's license. Have you ever noticed how many "John Smiths" there are in the phone book? Moreover, most of these transactions are cash payments. The patient wants no bill sent to his home or office. He will invariably show up for his next appointment, but it is impossible to reach *him*, since the address he has given doesn't exist. Our typical subject often visits a practitioner somewhat removed from his own habitat, since he doesn't want to run into anyone he knows. In any event, we begin vigorous treatment and urge him to refrain from intercourse.

Many of us remember the old custom in the military services prior to World War II when a venereal disease condition was often hidden by the serviceman and frequently resulted in severe disabling conditions. This was due to the fact that VD was punishable by additional time on duty without pay, so-called "bad time." This barbarous custom fortunately vanished, resulting in more prompt reporting and treatment of venereal conditions. We've come a long way out of the closet in our reporting of S.T.D. in general, which is a "must" in tracking down causative factors.

*Q. What can a teenager do if he thinks he's contracted VD?*

Head for his family physician or a public health agency. Public health records are confidential. The laws regarding invasion of privacy are very strict, and it is virtually impossible for a parent to check on a teenager.

As poor as I think sex education is in school, I also feel that we parents have done even a worse job, right at home, in speaking frankly to our children on how to protect themselves from the various diseases that are out there. By and large, the teenagers who get into trouble have not attended their sex education classes or have slept through them. Their parents have simply not done their jobs well at home. The oldest child in a family is most prone to get a venereal disease. He, in turn, then helps to educate his younger siblings when they reach the teen years.

*Q. If a man wants to bed a woman he doesn't know, is there any way to know if she is infected or not? Are there any danger signs?*

Three: (1) If she has a foul-smelling genital area, indicating poor hygiene or infection; (2) if she admits to having a profuse yellowish discharge or you happen to notice it on her underpants; and (3) if she admits to pain during intercourse.

If any of these clues are evident, do not pass "go." Do not collect the $200. Just get the hell out of there.

*Q. Which is the most common venereal disease today—syphilis or gonorrhea?*

Neither. Have you ever heard of NGU? It stands for "nongonnococcal urethritis" and has been called the "Cinderella of sexually transmissible infections" by one British expert ("The Cinderella Disease;" 1978, p. 73).

NGU is the most common sexually transmitted disease. According to the Center for Disease Control in Atlanta, somewhere between four and nine million Americans have it, whether they know it or not, and whether their doctors know it or not, since it is very difficult to diagnose.

The word *nongonococcal* means just that. When you examine a smear or culture for the presence of gonococci, there just aren't any. In the past, many doctors regarded this condition strictly as a urological inflammation that only occurs in men. In reality, it is a S.T.D. affecting both sexes.

It also seems to affect mostly the young, white, middle- and upper-middle-class swingers; those who indulge in a lot of sex. It is most common on the college campuses today.

*Q. What exactly is NGU?*

Let's go back to those two words again, *nongonoccal urethritis.* The channel that carries urine from the bladder is called the *urethra.* When that becomes inflamed, the condition is called *urethritis.* In gonorrhea, the culprit is a bacterium, the gonococcus bacterium. While NGU produces the same condition, we're still not sure how or why it starts except that it seems to be sexually transmitted.

Researchers are fairly sure that a tiny bacterium they have been tracking down called *Chlamydia trachomatis* is the culprit. This may be related to the same microbe that causes the disabling eye disease called *trachoma.* Seventy percent of NGU is due to chlamydia, while another microbe, *ureaplasma,* probably is responsible for the other 30 percent.

*Q. What are the symptoms? How do I know if I've got NGU?*

The symptoms are fairly innocuous. The male may feel some pain during urination or have a clear, watery, mucous discharge. In the female, there are usually no apparent symptoms.

The big problems occur if NGU is undiagnosed and left untreated. A man can end up with an inflamed epididymis. This gland carries sperm from the testes to the vas, and that transportation system is vital for fertility.

A woman may get an inflammation in the cervix or fallopian tubes, resulting in a blockage that could cause her to be sterile. If she is already pregnant, NGU can be passed on to her baby during birth, leading to possible lung or eye infections in the newborn infant.

*Q. How do you treat NGU? Is there a cure?*

I would first urge the average physician to do a little boning up on NGU, to make sure the difference between NGU and gonorrhea is understood. Gonorrhea usually responds to penicillin. NGU does not; there is no gonococcus. Once the smear shows its absence, your doctor should move ahead with oxytetracycline, then erythromycin.

Even in top research microbiology laboratories, it takes two weeks or more to make this differential diagnosis. So why wait? If the penicillin doesn't work, secondary treatment should start immediately.

*Q. If one member of a couple contracts NGU, should both be treated.*

Yes, indeed. S.T.D. means just that. It is transmittable. To prevent this ping-pong effect, the man should use a condom while both are under treatment.

*Q. When anyone used to mention VD, one thought of syphilis or gonorrhea. Now all I read about is herpes. What on earth is it?*

The official name is Herpes Simplex Virus, and there are two varieties involved.

Herpes Simplex I usually occurs above the navel. It's the kind you get with a cold sore or an irritation around the eyes or nose. In the past, it was not considered a sexually transmitted disease. But now, with more people engaging in oral-genital sex, it is not surprising to see this infection spreading to areas other than the mouth.

Herpes I usually responds slowly but easily to drying agents, such as camphor ice, which you can buy at the drugstore, or to a substance called Neutral Red. This latter medication, which is painted on the sores, should only be applied by a doctor at selected intervals. A type of photosynthesis occurs between Neutral Red dye and fluorescent light that seems to kill the virus.

Some material has been published stating that frequent use of Neutral Red may cause cancer in the affected area. That is why I feel strongly that the physician should be in charge of this procedure and should monitor how much and how often it is used.

For many years, there was a treatment vogue of administering small-pox vaccine at regular intervals, almost one month apart, over a period of a year in an effort to prevent Herpes Simplex I. This was based on the theory that there was some immunity conferred on individuals who had been vaccinated again and again, but this was of extremely limited value and has never been accepted as the treatment of choice.

*Q. When we talk about herpes, are we really talking about Herpes II?*

This is the strain that is driving both the patient and the physician up the wall.

You remember the old line, "I don't know how I got syphilis, since I never had intercourse. I must have picked it up on a toilet seat." As ridiculous as that claim sounded, it may very well hold true for Herpes II.

This virus hits below the waist, and it can be picked up anywhere and everywhere. This virus can even be on a table top, let alone a toilet seat. If people don't wash their hands or their bodies adequately prior to intercourse, it is not unlikely that this disease will be sexually transmitted.

Herpes II manifests itself in the male by means of sores over the tip of the penis or on the skin of the penile shaft. These are not to be confused with chancres—the hard red sores that come with syphilis and are not painful. Herpes sores are very painful.

In the female, it usually attacks the vaginal area, and, less frequently, the urethra.

*Q. How do I know if I have it?*

Oh, you'll know, all right. The man will have ulcerations and pain, usually in the mucous membrane just within the penis, on the uncircumcised undersurface of the foreskin, on the skin of the penis, or around the genital area. This will be one of the few times in his life when he dreads having an erection, because it hurts so much.

The woman will often have vaginal ulcerations that are extremely painful and itchy when the disease is active. For her as well, sex is an experience not to be cherished.

*Q. By "active," do you mean it comes and goes?*

That's what is so maddening about Herpes II. It may become inactive and retreat into a nerve plexus just below the small of your back, but it is never really gone. The virus just sits there and reappears at times when your body resistance is down. So, once you have contracted it, your chances of getting it again are great. You can almost be assured the disease will reappear. The highest incidence of repeat lesions is in the first year after contracting this condition. In subsequent years, it becomes less frequent.

It is highly communicable, so recurrence in one sexual mate will almost certainly reinfect the other. During "suspect" periods, a condom should be used to prevent herpes transmission back and forth. When the virus is "in full bloom" so to speak, you won't have this problem as a rule, since intercourse is usually too painful even to contemplate.

*Q. You mean there is no cure for Herpes II?*

There is no *permanent* cure as yet, but we certainly can alleviate the current epidemic and get people started on proper hygienic techniques.

A lot of herpes sufferers make the mistake of putting petroleum jelly on these lesions, which is the wrong thing to do. The sores are already moist. They need the reverse—to be dried out by exposure to air, light, and medicated powder.

The neutral red-fluorescent light procedure has proven more effective, under a doctor's supervision, for the male rather than the female patient. For the female, we usually use a topical agent, such as lidocaine, which is applied in an oily solution to kill the pain until the disease vanishes. We can usually teach the woman to apply this herself.

*Q. Does medical science have any idea why this disease has come to the forefront so much over the past decade?*

You are right when you used the word "forefront." Fifteen percent of the sexually active population today harbors the Herpes II virus! People are just making love more, both at younger *and* older ages. We're living in an era of sexual promiscuity and simply have more "players." The increase of Herpes II may also be associated with greater participation in oral sex.

*Q. What are the side effects of herpes?*

It can lead to cancer of the cervix, especially in those who start their sexual activities at a young age, with a variety of partners. This overexposure just increases the odds of getting the disease.

For example, who could be more overexposed than a prostitute? Close to *100 percent* of prostitutes show evidence of past or present herpes. This fact emphasizes the close relationship between sexual promiscuity and contracting the disease.

*Q. Is there any way to keep from getting herpes in the first place?*

If you're having intercourse with a casual partner who has a past history of herpes, suggest she use a contraceptive foam during intercourse. It seems to kill the herpes virus. Also, clean your genitals with soap and water afterward. Powder used on the genital area is not only pleasurable but also acts as an absorbing agent, drying out any secretion that may be left on your skin, thus acting as a reasonable preventive for the disease.

Several recent medical articles have appeared questioning the practice of washing after sexual exposure as a disease deterrent. I may be old-fashioned, but it seems more reasonable to me to remove all possible sources of infection from the skin and genital area.

*Q. If I seek medication for herpes, does the doctor have to trace down all my contacts and make out all those reports?*

No. Unlike syphilis and gonorrhea, herpes is like an unlisted phone number. You know it's there, but it is not reportable.

*Q. What are crabs? Are they in the S.T.D. family? Every time I ask somebody, I get a snicker.*

They are hardly a laughing matter. Crabs are tiny body lice that usually lodge in the pubic hair. Once embedded, they lay eggs called *nits.* They dig into your skin, leave little tracks and really itch like hell.

You can check for crabs by combing through your pubic hair onto a white piece of paper. In a bright light, you can see them jump off. Years ago, male or female, you would have to shave your genital area and then apply a terrible blue ointment. This became a sort of stigma. If you were blue, you had them. Later, DDT was used, until banned. Now there is a preparation called Qwell, available in either shampoo or ointment form, which can rid you of crabs in a few days.

The thing to remember is that crab lice can be transmitted even without contact. In other words, you *can* catch them on a toilet seat (especially a cracked one) or from contaminated linen, or clothing. However, they usually are transmitted sexually. Although the condom is the most effective preventative for most venereal diseases, it is obviously worthless against these little devils.

*Q. I know this sounds stupid, but could "warts" be sexually transmitted? I was living with a gal who had them. Now a wart has developed at the base of my penis and seems to be working its way to the tip.*

In the not so good old days, folklore suggested we could develop warts from picking up a frog. (Or was it a prince?) Then there was the school of thought that said your hand would break out in warts if you masturbated. So much for fiction. Let's get down to facts.

Yes, your wart is of viral origin. The condition here is related to herpes, but it is not the same virus. This one is called *condylomata,* and you could have very easily picked it up from your sexual companion.

Check into your urologist's office. He can paint it with a solution that will make it wither away. Several trips may be necessary, as he may have to apply subsequent "coats."

# Sexual Dysfunctions

## Premature Ejaculation

Why does a man come to a doctor? He may complain about a backache, headache, sour stomach, or gas. But no matter what his complaint is, about one-third of the time there is a sexual basis to his problem. For these men, "relief" is not spelled "R-o-l-a-i-d-s."

The most common sexual dysfunction of them all is premature ejaculation—the man climaxes too quickly. Once he gets upset about that—and who doesn't—of course he may get a backache, headache, sour stomach, or gas pains.

But how does it start? Premature ejaculation is usually a matter of poor training. Perhaps the man's earliest sexual experiences were with a prostitute who wanted to get the whole sex thing over with quickly: "Time is money. Wham bam, thank you, man." Or maybe he and his first sexual partner were afraid of being caught, so they had to employ the hurried hit-and-run technique. Perhaps his early sexual mates just didn't enjoy sex at all and urged him to hurry. This man is the type of individual who *always* had problems with ejaculating too quickly. Once he penetrates, he comes . . . and goes!!

Sadly, enough, once this pattern is set, each performance failure tends to make him even more anxious about the next. A snowball effect picks up with the passage of time, and failure begets failure.

Some men are accused of being premature ejaculators when they really are not. They arrive at orgasm in a normal length of time but may be coupled with a partner who takes forever. Others may experience temporary periods of premature ejaculation under certain circumstances such as being reintroduced to sex after a long period of abstinence or suddenly being overstimulated by the new woman on the block.

Whereas *all* men will experience impotence at one time or another, we may or may not ever suffer from premature ejaculation. If it happens to you once in a while, try these four options:

1. Make love a second time, or a third.
2. Grow older.
3. Have a few drinks.
4. Change positions.

*Q. Is premature ejaculation an organic problem or a psychological one?*

Premature ejaculation is in the *mind* about 70 percent of the time. There could be a physical cause such as a highly irritable ejaculatory duct, irritation of the prostate, or an inflammation of the bottom of the bladder. But let's rule those out, since they are readily diagnosed and quite easily treated.

Usually premature ejaculation is a conditioning problem, and there are two very simple techniques that can be of great help. At this point, the sexual partners are going to have to be aware of the part each one will have to play. A happy sex life takes two people. In training a man not to be a premature ejaculator, the woman has to be aware of her role, which is that of helper. She is being "used" in this situation, so her gratification will have to wait until her man is retrained.

The best of these retraining techniques are, basically, stop-and-go procedures. One exercise is called the Semens Technique. The man is aroused to a point just short of ejaculation. Then he is cooled off by stopping any foreplay or interplay. The use of ice or a cold washcloth to the genital area may be of great value here. Then the process starts again—arousal, then cooling off. This training may take several months, but you will notice a longer and longer period of time between initial excitation and ejaculation.

The other method that has shown good results is the Masters and Johnson Squeeze Technique.

This is somewhat horrendous to contemplate since it involves the woman applying great pressure to the penis during mounting excitation. She holds the man's penis in her hand, near the tip. Then, right before he is ready to come, with her thumb on the underside of the penis and two fingers above it, she very vigorously squeezes the penis. The penile squeeze doesn't cause the man to lose his erection but it does restrain ejaculation. (This is similar to pressing your finger below your nose to prevent a sneeze.)

Then, you go through the whole procedure again.

With either of these methods, a premature ejaculator can be trained to elongate the interval between stimulation and orgasm within a few months.

*Q. So all this takes place prior to actual penetration?*

Right. Either of these techniques must be used during foreplay. After all, once entrance has occurred, a woman can't very well grasp or squeeze the penis, which is already inside of her.

One final note. The squeeze method must be used exactly as I have described. Squeezing farther back, near the scrotum, will not retard ejaculation at all, especially after intercourse is already in progress.

*Q. I'm a premature ejaculator. What if my wife won't agree to go along with all of this.*

I'd want to talk to her, too, to try to find out what *she* wants out of your relationship? If she is perfectly satisfied with the way things are now, then she is probably not going to help. If she has been turned off by your inefficiency but wants sexual gratification, then we've got a chance for her cooperation. It gets down to three questions: "Does she want to improve her marriage? Does she like the status quo? Or does she want to terminate the relationship?"

*Q. I guess, like a lot of other men, this happens to me once in a while. When it does, I try to go on and satisfy my wife either orally or manually. But, at that point, she seems to resent it. Why?*

It's not your coming first that bothers her as much as the fact that she feels she is missing the physical closeness of intercourse, actual vaginal penetration. She feels cheated.

*Q. Is it possible for a man to be both impotent and a premature ejaculator? My husband has come to orgasm before he even gets an erection.*

In a baseball game, three strikes and you're out. He already has two of them. And yet it is not an uncommon situation.

We're really talking about the same group of nerves here. The tip of the penis, where most nerve ends are located, can be stimulated to orgasm without the blood supply increasing to create an erection. The fact that he can ejaculate indicates an intact nerve supply to the penis. Basically, it is a matter of sexual re-education by psychological counseling, using a couples technique. So all is not lost.

*Q. Are there any pills or shots you can take for premature ejaculation?*

No, there is no magical solution. If there were any that were uniformly successful, the manufacturer would make a fortune overnight. Some men feel that anesthetic jelly rubbed on the penis reduces sensitivity. Others believe that condoms help to hold them back. But there just isn't any quick sure cure.

The only pill that could slow a man down would be a sedative or tranquilizer. But that could interfere with his ability to have an erection in the first place. Remember, whenever you turn to chemistry, for every positive effect there is a negative side effect to be reckoned with.

*Q. But I have heard about drugs that can delay ejaculation. I think they are called anticholinergics.*

These have been used to control peptic ulcers in some patients. They may retard your ejaculation all right, because you may have a problem in getting an erection in the first place; in fact, you may lose the desire even to start the whole sexual process. Another unpleasant side effect could be an inability to expel your urine. I just can't balance the possible benefits of an anticholinergic against its risks under these circumstances.

*Q. My husband seems to have the reverse problem. He can get an erection all right but he can't ever ejaculate.*

This condition will bring a patient into a doctor's office fast—the man who is unable to have an ejaculation is often being pushed by his wife, who has taken the attitude that he obviously doesn't love her because he is not emitting within her. Maybe he doesn't love her and that may be why he is withholding his ejaculate from her. Perhaps he may erroneously feel he is practicing contraception by not ejaculating; in reality some sperm are present in the preclimactic fluid. He may believe that intercourse is dirty, or he may not want to be that deeply committed to any woman, especially his wife. He may be angry and feel that he is punishing her. He may truly not like women at all. He may feel that his wife represents his mother and that by not ejaculating he is not committing incest.

This type of situation presents a most serious psychological problem that requires intensive professional therapy for both husband and wife. Interestingly, many of these men can ejaculate with manual or oral stimulation.

# Impotence

*Every man experiences some periods of impotence during his lifetime.* Let me repeat that. Every one of us has experienced impotence—be it for an hour, a night, a week, a year, or longer.

What *is* impotence? Let's define it by using two other words: "disappointment" and "disaster." "Disappointment" is the *first* time you discover you can't have sex a *second* time. "Disaster" is the *second* time you find out you can't have sex the *first* time.

Being masculine is a never-ending battle, whether in your office or in your bed, a battle that must be fought day after day after day. When a man complains of impotence, I first try to ascertain what type he is talking about. Primary impotence is the inability to have sex—ever. The reasons behind this can be somewhat varied, he may have had an overly protective dominating mother or a Casper Milquetoast-type father. He may have been raised in a strict religious family, being brought up to believe that sex is dirty and should not be engaged in until after marriage.

Perhaps the first time he ever tried sex, he failed, which may have been due to a number of things: squalid surroundings, a woman who wasn't appreciative, fear of interruption, and so on.

Secondary impotence, which is far more common, means that there has been a recent failure rate of more than 25 percent during attempted intercourse after previous sexual competence. This type of patient is far more responsive to treatment.

*Q. I'm sure I fit into that second group. I'm just an average forty-year-old married type with a wife and two kids. But lately I just can't get it up. What can be done for me?*

Since many cases of impotence are psychological, first I would want to find out about your background. How old were you when you had your first sexual experience? It appears that the later you bloom the earlier you fade.

I would want to know how long you have been married and whether you still find your wife attractive. Have you found that you are impotent only with your wife? What time of day do you usually make love? Do you like what you do for a living? Do you have money worries? Could you be a latent homosexual?

If the answers to these questions indicate that there is, indeed, a psychological base to your impotence, I would prescribe large doses of tender loving care from your doctor *and* your wife. If this doesn't work, in-depth psychotherapy may be indicated.

*Q. What if I answer all your questions with flying colors and I still can't get an erection?*

Then we turn to the *physical* aspects. Do you shave daily? Insufficient or sparse hair distribution could indicate hormonal problems.

Is your penis warm or cold? If it is cold, we might look for an interruption in the blood flow, which could have resulted from arteriosclerosis or a previous surgical procedure. Or it could indicate a blood disorder such as leukemia or sickle-cell disease.

Do you have feeling in your penis? If there are changes in sensation, you may have early multiple sclerosis or some other degenerative neurological disease.

Are you an alcoholic? Ten million adult Americans are. Alcohol exaggerates previously existing depressions and fears, adds body weight, decreases sensitivity, and reduces sexual drive.

Do you have cancer or some other energy-sapping condition like anemia? Are you afflicted with severe kidney failure, such as uremic poisoning? Many dialysis patients become impotent.

If you have answered "no" to all of these questions, I'd first suggest a rectal examination of your prostate gland to make sure it is OK. Then, a series of blood tests would be indicated to evaluate your total body function and hormone balance. Those same tests would also indicate whether or not you have diabetes.

*Q. I've recently learned I have diabetes. Could that be the reason I have had very little interest in sex?*

It's quite possible. About half of all diabetics are impotent at some point. One of the primary tests we do on a patient complaining of impotence is a glucose tolerance test. We have thus uncovered many cases of unsuspected diabetes. There is no direct relationship between impotence and the severity of the diabetes, the length of time you've had it, or if it's been brought under control.

*Q. I don't understand what diabetes has to do with impotence.*

In diabetics, the blood vessels of the body lose their elasticity. They become somewhat hardened and thickened, so that the blood flow through them is reduced. Also, scar tissue formation at nerve endings, and nerve degeneration, cause failure in sexual impulse transmission.

In the penis, this results in a poor erection or none at all.

*Q. Is it possible for a man to be impotent and still get nighttime erections?*

Yes, and as a matter of fact, there are some interesting findings now being reported from various university sleep centers. A fascinating new apparatus called a Peter Meter is being used to measure nighttime erections. There is a fine wire loop that is placed around the base of the penis. This gauge is hooked up to an electronic recording device, so when a man gets an erection at night it is tracked on the recorder. In another room, a signal light goes on, or a bell rings, depending on the specific test series. Then, a trained observer quietly removes the patient's bedclothes so as not to awaken him and observes the size and firmness of the erection. As many as sixty erections in one man have been recorded in a single night. The normal male has four to six erections in the course of a night.

This is an expensive procedure, however, costing around three thousand dollars for one night's test in the sleep clinic. The patient can rent such a device and try it at home, provided his sexual partner is willing to stay up waiting for the light to go on or the bell to ring.

*Q. Why would a man want to subject himself to all this?*

Simply to find out if his impotence is organic or psychological. Often we cannot find an organic cause for a patient's problem, and this would be one of the final tests prior to suggesting psychotherapy or a penile implant. This test proves positively whether or not a man is truly able to function sexually. You cannot be sexually intact just some of the time.

*Q. Do impotence and just plain growing old go hand in hand?*

Indeed not. All kinds of important factors may play a part here. Are you in a dull, boring relationship? Do you feel you lack personal privacy? Are you disappointed in the realization that you may not attain your career goals? Are you no longer needed, either by your family or by your employer? Is your self esteem at low ebb?

Let's look at the physical aspect. As men get over the age of sixty-five, there is a definite decline in the measurable serum testosterone levels. Between puberty and approximately age fifty-five, the level is fairly constant. But, remember, Senator Strom Thurmond fathered a child at the age of seventy-six. So you're really never sexually "over the hill."

Past studies do show, however, that as one ages intercourse remains fairly frequent up to the age of fifty-five. Then it begins to decline abruptly. One of the biggest reasons for this has nothing to do with the man at all. It has to do with the lack of a willing sexual partner.

*Q. Maybe I am the exception. I'm fifty-two now and my sex life has never been better.*

Good for you. Actually, I have been painting much too gloomy a picture. Look at the advantages of sex and age. As a man matures, his erections may take longer to achieve but, when he does engage in sex, he finds he can last much longer before orgasm occurs. He has conditioned his ejaculatory response. A younger man is more often "quick like a bunny," because he is more easily aroused but less controlled.

Quite happily, as you get a bit older, you'll find that your acquired finesse over the years has made you a far better lover.

*Q. I don't know whether I'm impotent or not. Every time my wife and I make love, I've been getting sort of a weak erection. Then afterward, I'm bushed for two days. What's wrong with me?*

Probably nothing. This reaction may involve your bringing your job home with you. You are tired. You are anxious. Each semierection tends to build up in your mind thus producing the next semierection.

It takes energy to have an erection. It takes energy to have intercourse. As for feeling bushed afterwards—this is quite normal. I'd suggest you plan your next encounter on a weekend morning, when you're rested and have all the time in the world to stay in bed afterward. Also, if you usually assume the male superior position, reverse it for a change. Have your wife get on top and let her take the initiative.

*Q. So my wife can play an important part in my lack of interest in sex?*

It happens frequently, especially with the menopausal woman who, either through disability or lack of interest, turns her husband away. There is also the woman who picks bedtime as fight time. This creates a situation where the man is most likely to become sexually dysfunctional.

*Q. Is there a male equivalent to menopause?*

A lot has been made recently of "middle-aged rebellion" or "the beaten dog syndrome," but I can't support any theory of a male menopause. Men have a whole combination of events going on: lack of personal and business growth, financial pressures of having children in college, and, perhaps, a growing dissatisfaction with a spouse.

Actually, during this period many a husband is repelled by his wife. Perhaps he feels his wife's breasts are too large or too small, or that she is too fat or too thin. If the wife is managing the household while the husband is in the work force, he may find himself surrounded by young, trim, chic twenty-year-olds. And he may still be hung up on that mythical American correlation between young, firm bodies and good sex.

A great deal of sexual mismatching becomes apparent among married couples after the age of forty. One partner may be a "night person" addicted to Johnny Carson or the late late show while the other partner believes in "early to bed, early to rise." This is the period when we often see a change in sleeping habits from a double bed to twin beds or to separate bedrooms.

*Q. We're almost at the separate bedroom stage, because we don't seem to like the same things anymore. What can we do?*

Maybe *one* of you never *did* like the same things to begin with. During your courting days, you were both playing the "part" of lover. But many years have passed. Who has time for games anymore? At last you start being your true self, only to get hit with lines like, "My, how you've changed!" Perhaps, you haven't changed at all. But finally, you're being honest enough to admit you enjoy the Sunday professional football game much more than the opera, and Rigoletto gives way to the Raiders.

As far as separate bedrooms are concerned, think of how your *sexual* habits have changed through the years. That wild early experimentation slowly deteriorated into predictable, mechanized monotony. Oral-genital sex gave way to the old "he's on top, she's on the bottom" syndrome every other Tuesday. What's the answer? You must vary your lives. Start by changing the Big Three: time, place, and position. And one more thing. Get that damn television set out of the bedroom. Trying to cram sex between two used-car commercials and a station identification just isn't worth the effort.

*Q. Is it true that the successful corporate executive puts all his efforts into his job and is not much interested in sex?*

Quite the *opposite*. It seems that the more successful you are, the more sexually active you are going to be. You are also more likely to engage in extramarital sex. One-third of all men who earn over $50,000 a year are probably playing around. Men who have more than four drinks a day are commonly involved in extramarital sex. If they are traveling men and spend at least one day a week away from home, they're also more apt to be unfaithful.

*Q. I am divorced, in my late forties, and have recently been dating some liberated women. Frankly, they scare the hell out of me. Talk about instant impotence—I've got it.*

We are now seeing an immense caseload of men like you who are very uptight about the rise of the sexually adventurous feminist. The younger man is coping better, since he has grown up with women who talk openly about sex. In the older man, having his date discuss who is good in bed and who isn't causes raised eyebrows and unraised penises.

Today it is often the woman who is calling the shots as to intercourse: frequency, position, and sexuality in general. Many a man can no longer handle it. He is retreating, and he's sure that something is wrong with him, and he doesn't know what. There really is nothing wrong with him. He just has to make peace with himself. Times have changed.

He may have grown up with the philosophy that you don't even kiss until the third date. Now he is involved with a woman who is almost a total stranger and with whom he can't talk over past events, because there weren't any. He'd like to develop some sort of personal relationship, while she is suggesting bed. While he is still trying to establish dialogue, she is ready for the sack. He is caught between two conflicting sets of values, a generation gap, and a set of unrealistic expectations. It is not at all unusual these days to hear the male equivalent of "Not tonight, dear, I have a headache."

*Q. Hell, I'm not running around with any chicky babies. I've got enough trouble at home with my wife demanding her sexual rights.*

Today's woman has been bombarded with hundreds of magazine articles stating, in so many words, that if she is experiencing anything less than total ecstasy every time, there is something wrong with her love life or with her life's love. She is reading articles like "How to Express Your Real Feelings Without Hurting Your Marriage," "Is It Better with a Younger Man?" "Should a Total and Complete Orgasm Be Part of Your Household Guarantee?" "Will My Husband Be Good for Ten Years Or 100,000 Miles, Whichever Comes First?" "Is It True That 'Doing It' in a Bathtub Full of Jello Is a Turn-on?" (Perhaps, only if it's lime Jello.)

Can anyone answer all those monumental questions and still keep the husband sane and reasonably content? None of us is perfect all of the time. Sex is not perfect all of the time.

*Q. I recently met a girl at a party who really turned me on. We went to her place, and I had an erection that wouldn't quit—until she took her clothes off. Then I saw that she was overweight and sort of repulsive. Sure enough, it was "bye-bye erection."*

Although to many men a woman remains sexy only as long as she *keeps* her clothes on, the ideal sexual playmate is rare to find, except as a navel-stapled centerfold in a well-known magazine. Fantasy is fun but you must develop a more mature sexual attitude—unlike that of a movie, years ago, called "The Immoral Mr. Teas." In that film, the hero got his jollies by mentally picturing as naked every woman he saw. Based on that rather immature concept, try reversing the procedure and picture your naked woman clothed. Remember, you don't have to be a Greek god or goddess to enjoy good sex!

*Q. About a year ago, my husband had a heart attack. He seems fine now, but he won't come near me for fear of another attack.*

I don't know how many times we doctors have to reassure a cardiac patient that it's OK to have intercourse: "No, sir, you are not going to die when you make love." In fact, sexual activity improves health. The oxygen expended in having intercourse is about equal to climbing a flight of stairs, slowly.

There is, however, one interesting statistic: about 0.9 percent of all people who have coronary artery disease *do* expire during love making. But most of *those* men were in the middle of having extramarital intercourse, probably at a business convention, away from home. Conquest of the unknown often involves more frequent and more vigorous intercourse.

I would advise men to stick to home cooking. You are on firmer ground when you make love with your regular, understanding partner.

*Q. After seeing the movie "Coming Home" with Jane Fonda and Jon Voigt, I wondered if this type of thing is really going on.*

Yes indeed. Spinal cord injuries are extremely common, not only with the war wounded but also with motorcycle and automobile accidents. Men with these injuries are partially or totally paralyzed and have both physical limitation and discomfort. They first experience psychological shock, followed later by anger, despair, depression, and strong feelings of inadequacy, particularly in regard to sexual matters. Formerly paraplegics were advised to "forget it" as far as sex was concerned. Everyone supposes that these men just do not have sex. They, of course, do fear abandonment or rejection by their sexual partner. Sexual response of a paraplegic is largely dependent upon desire and a willing partner. These men use sexual ability as a redefinition of their masculinity. Once proven, their self esteem is restored. We believe that anything goes sexually, that is functionally possible. Sexual achievement is as important as breathing to the spinal cord injury man.

*Q. What about people who are seriously ill, and hospitalized for long periods of time. Can they learn to have sex again?*

Of course. Since the sexual model that we remember from our youth does not feature the severely ill or injured man, these people feel that they are only "half a man" because they cannot fantasize their sexual performance as able bodied individuals. They feel guilty because they don't possess ideal bodies. Yet it is usually their worries that cause the majority of their sexual problems, not the basic illness itself. Many health professionals feel that sex is an inappropriate concern for these men. In point of fact, sex is one of their major preoccupations, secondary only to their ability to re-establish their mobility and resume their working life.

The patient should bring up the question of sexuality himself and be supported in obtaining answers to his questions. Performance expectation must be realistically adjusted to actual physical capability. This may be dependent upon stimulation by sight, odor, touch or taste. It is important that these men should no longer be relegated to a hopeless future without sexual fulfillment.

# Part Four

# How It All Adds Up— and Other Considerations

## Sex for Seniors

YEARS AGO, IN the days of big-time network radio, there was a program called "The Shadow." Every week, the announcer would open the show by saying in a deeply resonant voice, "Who knows what evil lurks in the heart of man? The Shadow knows. . . ." If you delete the word *evil* and substitute the word *fear*, you come pretty close to describing man in this latter part of the twentieth century. He lives in a society that constantly equates youth with virility. To him, aging is regarded as a dread disease to be fought off. Yet the alternative to aging is dying young.

Today's man leads a life of fear. In his puberty years, he fears the unknown. During adolescence, he fears he may fail in his clumsy early attempts at love making. Actually, he never loses this performance anxiety. So from puberty to senility, man must prove himself over and over again. It is almost like hearing "I know you bought me a new house in June, a new fur coat in July, and a new sports car in August. But here it is, September, and what have you done for me lately?"

Throughout his lifetime, at one time or another, man may fear the sexually aggressive woman, the sexually passive woman, or the super-competent woman who doesn't need him to lean on at all. He may fear his proposal of marriage may be rejected—or accepted, trapping him into marriage. How does his penis compare with others? And, above all, he may always fear being made a cuckold.

An older man commonly feels threatened by the competitive young man on his way *up*, both in bed and in earning a living. Money troubles can totally destroy a man's active sex life. Dr. Sophia Kleegman (Cilento and Felshman, 1978, pp. 26–27) recalls that during the 1929 market crash "penises dropped faster than the stocks on Wall Street." There is a definite correlation between financial pressures and sexual performance.

Certainly, man fears the unknown. From each moment to the next, all of us like to know exactly where we stand and what to expect. Even though surprises can be fun, some are not. So, we don't want too many of them.

During the passage of a man's middle years, he may find that outside business pressures have dramatically lessened his sex drive. Perhaps, around the age of fifty, he has reached another level in his life. By now, he is already the president of his company, or knows he never will be. Adjustments have to be made. Family connections must be reestablished, but until his children have left the nest maybe his wife isn't quite ready. When it finally does come down to just the two of them alone, we often see a complete shift in relationships. Suddenly, the woman who is liberated from running a household, or holding a job, wants to give all of her attention to her husband. She expects him to "come out and play," but maybe he just isn't interested. For years, she has been too tired. Then, when she wakes up, he has drifted off.

If he just thinks back to his younger days he'll remember there were always times when he failed to live up to the sexual standards he had fantasized for himself. Now he has a chance to move forward again and reestablish a relationship with his wife. In fact, he may find himself revitalized now that his working years are over.

There is no special age at which one becomes old. One man is young at sixty, another old at forty. Sure, sex may be engaged in less frequently, but the male does not simply lose his facility for erection at any given time. His sexual capacity is changing, rather than declining.

To many outsiders, sex in the aged seems inappropriate. Elderly men and women are often lonely and sexually frustrated. Yet the younger generation doesn't help them very much by putting all kinds of social obstacles in their path. The older folks embarrass their children. Well, too bad! It's time to dump these Victorian beliefs and look at life as it really is. While our seniors may not have as strong a sexual desire as before, it is most certainly still there.

As far as health is concerned in later years, sex is not a dangerous activity. If you're well enough to take a walk, you're well enough to have sex.

As Alex Comfort once said, "The only thing age has to do with sexual performance is that the longer you love, the more you learn." (Quoted in Katchatourian and Lunde, 1975.)

*Q. I still enjoy sex, but my erection isn't as firm or as good.*

This is a common complaint. In my office, I hear "my erection is only 80 percent of what it used to be," or 60 percent, or whatever. Don't worry about what it used to be. Just accept the way things are now and be thankful you have *some* percent. Enjoy. Playing the numbers game is the first self-defeating step toward impotence.

It reminds me of the story of the ninety-year-old man who thought he was getting stronger, because for the first time in his life he could bend his erect penis.

*Q. I don't consider myself to be one of your Victorian types. But lately I've been reading about seniors living together and not getting married. Isn't that living in sin?*

They are, indeed, cohabitating without the benefit of clergy. Is it scandalous? Hardly!

Let's look at the hard facts. We live in an inflationary era. The cost of living is going out of sight. Without *both* Social Security checks, these people just can't make it financially. If they marry, one of them has to give up his or her income.

Age brings wisdom in this regard. These seniors know by now that dollars bring security to a relationship. Love is fine, but you still have to buy groceries and pay the rent.

*Q. You mean these old people are having sex?*

Sure they are. Maybe it's not the wild orgiastic sex of their younger years, but there is still a driving need for affection, for closeness, for involvement with another human. As with all the rest of us, what is life all about if it doesn't include sharing love and personal feelings?

When a couple gives up sex, they also seem to give up all other forms of physical affection. Perhaps they are now enjoying sex without orgasm. But it still involves kissing, fondling, touching, and penetration. Sex without climax is still sex, another way of reassuring each other of their love.

I think it is time to realize that sex among seniors is going to be an ever-increasing occurrence. Our changing demographics now show that vast percentages of our population will soon be moving into their "Golden Years."

*Q. Let's get back to the middle-aged woman. If she gets turned off to sex during her menopausal years, does her husband also?*

He usually does, unless he takes a mistress or masturbates. Remember our byword—"use it or lose it." Those menopausal years can mean the end of or a renewing of their relationship. If they both turn asexual because of abstinence, chances are they may never regain their interest in sex.

*Q. Maybe I'm the woman you are talking about. I am several years into menopause, and I really couldn't care less about making love. Can anything be done?*

I think I first better point out how the menopausal years have changed. Menopause now arrives later in a woman's life, usually around the age of fifty. If untreated, it can last for many years.

You sound like a woman who is going through it *cold turkey.* That means hot flashes, mood changes, bitchiness, and so on. Were I in your position, I'd probably feel cold about sex, too.

But also, if I were you I'd look into hormonal supplements like estrogen. You may actually prolong menopause, but you will prolong your youth, too. A woman who takes estrogen is going to keep up her vaginal lubrication. Her skin is going to look nicer and have fewer wrinkles. She is going to be physically more attractive, to herself and to those around her. I have found that the woman who remains young and attractive, by virtue of hormonal intake, is just a happier person.

She is not going to get that widow's hump that appears on the back of her neck. You've seen the women who walk with their necks a bit forward? This "widow's hump" is caused by thinning or softening of her bones, particularly in her neck area. An accordion-like effect occurs with the front of the bones becoming more compressed than the back, thus producing the deformity.

*Q. If I do take estrogen, will I ever be able to get to the point where I can give it up, or will I be committed to it for the rest of my life?*

You can probably give it up eventually and not get the hot flashes anymore, or the mood swings, but actually, many women stay on small doses of estrogen forever to support their bodies.

*Q. What about the side effects, the tendency to get cancer, that I keep hearing about?*

If there is a history of cancer of the female organs in yourself or your family, or, if there have been lumps in your breast, stay away from hormone supplements, in large or small doses.

For the rest of you, the choice is yours. Either you make the choice of staying youthful and moist, or you accept the aging process with its own potential side effects.

*Q. My wife and I haven't had sex in years. Is it too late for us? We're in our sixties, and I don't feel like rolling over and playing dead quite yet.*

This is one of the classic confrontations between desire and performance. When coitus has been abandoned for a long time, it is still possible for older men and women to return to a satisfying sex life. I, first, recommend a complete physical examination for both partners. Then I think it is time for what I call sex education for Gram and Gramp, therapy to relieve tensions and anxieties.

One of the effective ways to improve erectile ability in the aging man is to alter activity patterns. Instead of trying to get it together late at night, how about in the morning, when you both are fresh? Many men, in their retirement years, have no pressing daily schedule. How about sex at nine in the morning, and why not change your usual position?

We also counsel couples in how to vary their methods of stimulation. Potency may be improved, with the cooperation of both partners. The older male, who once could be quickly aroused now often needs help by manipulation. Sure, the encounter may take more time. But isn't time what you both, at last, have plenty of?

*Q. I'd like to have more sex with my wife, but I just can't feel anything anymore. Her vagina is too big. Is this a normal problem for seniors?*

Unfortunately, yes. As we get older, *all* our muscles get flabby, and the ones around the vagina are no exception. If your wife were younger, I'd suggest a surgical repair. But, in her older age group, the risk outweighs the gain. She might try a series of exercises, contracting and relaxing her pelvic muscles. When done faithfully, they will work to give her a tighter, snugger vagina. Another suggestion is for her to hold her hips tighter around you when you enter her.

*Q. My wife experiences a lot of pain when she tries to tighten her hips. Why?*

The number one cause for sexual dysfunction in an older man or woman is the disability resulting from arthritis. Crippled joints are just not pliable. Your wife seems to fit into this category. She probably can neither open nor close her legs without a great deal of discomfort, making intercourse most unpleasant for her, as well as for you. Women, more than men, tend to develop marked mechanical limitation of hip motion. This handicap may result in depression and reactive hostility, deteriorating a formerly close relationship. It's important to choose the position best tolerated by the affected joints. With sexual activity, many arthritics not only feel better but also are relieved of pain. However, it may require warmup preparation with massage or locally applied heat before intercourse. If intercourse is impossible, alternative means of sexual gratification must be considered.

*Q. Since he retired, my husband has put on forty pounds and just doesn't seem interested in sex anymore. Is this customary?*

Yes because obesity breeds shame. He's unhappy with himself, and can't stand looking in the mirror at what appears to be a bloated body and a tiny penis. Fat men have great difficulty finding a suitable position for intercourse, and I'm sure you're not overjoyed in having that overweight on top of you.

It seems that with maturity, physical activity slows down and so does one's metabolism—the ability to make use of food. With overeating and particularly overdrinking, everything turns to fat. Try reducing his portions of food and booze. Tell him once he loses pounds, he will gain interest.

*Q. My husband is not only disinterested in sex, he's disinterested in everything. What's going on?*

At a point in later middle age, a man will often pick up the morning paper, ignore the news and sports, and turn directly to the obituary column. He wants to see which of his friends are still around. He is going through a period of self-evaluation, wondering how much of life is left for him, and of what quality it will be. He may try to self-destruct in a number of ways, including the overuse of booze. If he feels he has nothing to look forward to, he may suffer through periods of irritability, fatigue, and insomnia.

Men in this age group associate loss of sexual adequacy with loss of identity: "Who am I? Where am I?" Losing his erection is like losing his job. He has had both for a long time. These men become sexual dropouts—spectators, rather than participants.

You have a big job here. He needs support and reassurance. You should "love him up" like you never have before.

*Q. Whenever I watch TV, the men are all young and handsome, and the women are young and beautiful. My wife and I are in our late fifties. Lately, we both have started looking old but continue to feel young. My hair is thinning and graying rapidly. Any comments about our considering plastic surgery?*

Have it. And, how about a hair transplant as well? If you want a hairpiece, get a good one. If you want to dye what's left of your gray hair, do it. If you want cosmetic surgery to remove the bags from under your eyes, go ahead—both of you. Like so many other things, face lifts have finally come out of the closet. Psychologically you'll get a lift too, especially every time you look at each other, as well as into the mirror.

*Q. You mentioned changing our pattern of living. With our kids gone, we are wondering if we need this big house anymore. Can changing our whole lifestyle improve our sex life?*

I see it happen all the time. Changing your lifestyle, for example moving to a smaller place in a warmer climate, really can get things going again. It gives you both a new challenge: a new nest to furnish, new friends to make—most of whom will be in your own age bracket.

Let us say you sell the old house. You will still retain its good memories, but you are able to eliminate its liabilities. Often a couple will find that their house has become too much of a burden. Maybe the husband no longer wants to fight the battle of the weeds. It has become too much for him, physically. Perhaps he prefers to play golf every day, or they both want to travel more.

There gets to be a "time for us" point in your life. This is one way to establish such an important priority.

I find more and more people going into "turnkey" operations— condominiums or townhouses—where several houses share recreational facilities. If the couple wants to take off, they can rent their unit and not have to worry about its upkeep. Management takes care of all that. Keeping up with the Joneses gives way to what pleases the two of you most. You'll be amazed how much tension you have eliminated, how much enjoyment your new life promises.

*Q. I have heard that one of the problems of aging is that a man has a limited amount of semen in his lifetime. Thus in later years he fears it will run out.*

Absolute poppycock. If that were true, no one would ever masturbate, fearing that he would be squandering his predetermined supply of semen. A man may ejaculate less frequently and in smaller amounts as he gets older, but that has nothing to do with any kind of quota system.

# The Gay Life

No book on male sexuality today can or should omit those who have chosen the homosexual way of life. According to current estimates, 10 percent of American men today are open, avowed, "out of the closet" homosexuals. How many more are latent, bisexual, or gay but still hidden "in the closet," no one knows.

One man in ten has publicly declared himself homosexual. He prefers other men as lovers. To some of these individuals, gayness is almost a religion. If you were to ask these individuals if they were Catholic, Protestant, or Jewish, most likely they would answer, "We are gay." Former civil rights leader and Episcopal priest, Malcolm Boyd (1978), expressed it this way: "Gayness *is* my ethnicity." Most gays believe that their lifestyle is something they were born with, something that is beyond their control, and that their paths to happiness involve accepting themselves and being accepted by others as they are.

The more a homosexual comes out of the closet, the more he overtly moves within gay circles. Says the Reverend Malcolm Boyd (1978): "Otherwise, it would be necessary for me to coexist in two quite different worlds. Did I have sufficient energy to do this?"

Once he openly declares himself, the path of least resistance for the homosexual leads him to be one person in one world. In addition to sexual pursuits, like cruising or frequenting gay baths or bars, he may find that his everyday life includes dealing with a gay travel agent, going on a gay tour, insuring his car with a gay insurance agent, and buying his house from a gay realtor. He tends to withdraw, bit by bit, from the heterosexual world, feeling perhaps that it only gives him ridicule or rejection. He can also tire of constantly trying to explain why he is like he is.

He tires of trying to answer those who claim that they can make him "right" again; those who assume that the gay regrets his sexual proclivities and would jump at the chance of being "cured." Since the average homosexual doesn't consider himself to be sick, what's to cure? Years ago, the American Psychiatric Association announced that homosexuals should no longer be considered ill, nor should they be deemed social misfits.

Additionally, the gay has had it with many heterosexual doctors who look down their noses at gays as patients. These doctors lecture to them that their real sickness is their homosexuality. Many doctors are unable to properly diagnose diseases and injuries that are special to the homosexual world. For example, if a patient told a straight doctor that he had diarrhea and stomach pain, the physician might check him for a viral disease or appendicitis. A gay doctor might look for a parasitic disease called *giardiasis*, usually connected with oral-anal sexual contact.

A gay patient feels most comfortable with a gay doctor but probably has had trouble finding one. Nationwide, of some 400,000 physicians, 13,000 have now officially come out of the closet and are making themselves known. In Northern California, the San Francisco Chronicle reported that more than 200 doctors formed the first actual organization of homosexual doctors, complete with telephone hotline. Perhaps we'll get to the point where, under "Physicians" in the Yellow Pages, along with "internists" and "allergists," "gays" will be listed.

There has been tons of material written on the so-called reasons for a man to choose the homosexual life. Could it be the emotional strains of early childhood, the dominant mother-weak father syndrome, or lack of female companionship about the time of puberty, when a boy seems to develop a fixation on other boys? If this is the type of information you are seeking, look to other sources.

In this chapter, my aim is to examine the gay male as a human being and to answer questions about his sexuality and physical problems.

*Q. I can attest to the fact that I've been treated like a second-class citizen in the straight medical world. But if I can't find a gay doctor in my community, what can I do?*

Fortunately, things are changing for the better, especially in large metropolitan areas, where there is a substantial homosexual population. A lot of medical "straights" are staying current on what to expect in the way of gay patients' complaints. Of course, this demands candor between the doctor and his gay patient, as well as familiarity with homosexual habits. The doctor has to know something of the lifestyle of his patient, whatever his sexual preference.

For example, if a man comes in with a reddened, irritated penis, and if I think he is gay, I would assume he has the Princeton Rub. This condition comes from body rubbing. If the penis is rubbed over a particularly hairy part of the body, it can become most irritated. If a straight doctor looks at this and wonders what it can be, he must be willing to seek advice. Believe me, it is not that difficult these days to call a gay colleague and say, "I've seen something I've never seen before. What do you make of it?" Admittedly, gay doctors are no better or worse than the rest of us. They, too, require specialists to back them up in certain instances. But it is reassuring to know that help is there if you ask for it.

*Q. This may sound stupid, but I don't really know how homosexuals make love.*

According to the latest Kinsey Institute findings reported by Bell & Weinberg there are, several different sexual techniques. The most frequently used technique is performing oral sex on his partner or having it performed on him. Then, in a decreasing order of incidence: "being masturbated by his partner followed by masturbating him, performing anal intercourse or having anal intercourse performed on him, and, reaching orgasm through body rubbing" (Bell and Weinberg, 1978, p. 107).

*Q. I have to go to a straight doctor once in a while, and I never admit to him that I am gay. I have a standing in the community, and I don't want his spreading the word about me.*

Patient-physician confidentiality should preclude that. However, when I see the voters of a liberal state like California voting on whether school boards should have the power to fire gay teachers, I can understand your uneasiness. Suppose the patient is a teacher, and the doctor has a good friend on the school board. It would be inexcusable of him to say to his friend, "Guess who has oral gonorrhea?" But I suppose it could happen, if the physician's politics or big mouth got the better of him.

Perhaps you should visit a doctor in another community and pay cash —no bills. There is no quick cure for this most unfortunate situation that you describe. It's a shame. Stay proud!

*Q. Are homosexuals more prone to sexually transmitted disease?*

Yes. Vastly so. The new Kinsey survey and other reports show that 34 percent have contracted some form of S.T.D. once or twice, and 28 percent three times or more. This adds up to the fact that over 60 percent of the homosexual community will end up with a sexually transmitted disease, probably more than once.

The Center for Disease Control now attributes over 45 percent of *all* early syphilis cases in the United States to gay men, 28 times higher than in the heterosexual population. There is a higher incidence of gonorrhea, with 90 percent of the infected males developing the characteristic symptoms of discharge, penile swelling, and balanitis (an irritation of the foreskin). For every case reported, health officials estimate there are three to four unreported cases which are, therefore, untreated, causing an epidemic. We are seeing both syphilis and gonorrhea of the mouth from oral copulation. Genital herpes is rampant.

These extremely high S.T.D. rates are not surprising when you realize that some homosexuals may have hundreds of partners during their
lifetimes. One "bug" can course through many bodies. Let's face it,
promiscuity breeds every known form of sexually transmitted disease
which causes physical disabilities that continue to astound us. This
leads us back to the gay patient-straight doctor relationship. Where
the straight doctor has put down the gay patient and made him feel
like the repulsive minority, the homosexual has often thought, "Who
needs this hassle?" So he has avoided going to a doctor for urgently
needed care.

*Q. Why do you keep talking about homosexual men? Wouldn't lesbians
have the same problems?*

In no way. A gay woman's S.T.D. rate is only slightly higher than that
of a celibate. The lesbian goes through her life with fairly long, stable
relationships.

*Q. My main concern is not my gay lifestyle but that horrible gonorrhea
rate. How often should I get checked for S.T.D.?*

First off, you can forget about that annual checkup right now. The
sexually active homosexual male should have an S.T.D. check *at least
every three months,* preferably more often. And I mean everything
checked—rectal smear, throat smear, a smear of the fluid within the
penis, and a blood test for syphilis.
Infectious hepatitis affects 90 percent of the gay community at some
time or another. This liver disease causes a blockage of the ducts that
secrete bile. As the bile is held back in the body, the patient feels
tremendous lassitude and fatigue. In advanced cases, he develops jaun-
diced eyes, or his whole body can turn yellow.
A stool examination for possible parasites may show amoebic dysentery, pinworm, or *Giardia lambia.* Anal warts are also common in this
sexually active group (Fenwick, 1978).

*Q. How would I know if I had gonorrhea of the rectum?*

Under normal circumstances, you wouldn't. That's why that examination, at least every three months, is so vital. The difficulty is that the
smear, which is very accurate in diagnosing gonorrhea of the penis, is

unreliable in detecting oral or rectal gonorrhea. Here, we have to depend on a culture, the results of which will not be known for forty-eight hours.

*Q. You stated that 10 percent of the men today are "out of the closet" homosexuals. Yet didn't the original Kinsey Report state that one in three men have had a homosexual experience?*

It was higher than that. Closer to 37 percent had an encounter by the age of forty. But one encounter does not a lifestyle make.

Many young boys, during puberty, experiment with homosexuality in "gang jerk-offs," masturbating one another. Again, this does not mean a gay life ahead.

Many older men, after being married for years and raising a family, will suddenly leave their wives and announce that they are gay. Why? Perhaps, they reevaluated themselves, felt that their sexual preferences had changed, that their marriages had become dull, or that they simply didn't like women anymore.

Then there are those who claim the best of both worlds: the bisexuals. About 3 percent of the male population seems to fit in this category. The bisexual is, basically, a sexual adventurer, likely to engage in group sex, orgies, you name it. Unless his female partner is similarly inclined, it is tough to keep up with him. Although the bisexual probably prefers a man as a lover, he will often marry for social acceptance.

*Q. I've heard that homosexuality is determined from birth, that if a boy is going to be gay he is born that way.*

Dr. Burton White, the famous Harvard researcher on preschoolers and author of *The First Three Years*, would not support your theory. He says that even if a young male child prefers dolls to fire trucks, that is absolutely no indication he will grow up homosexual.

I hate to disappoint you, but there is no definitive answer as to why a young man will prefer a gay lifestyle. Neither doctor nor psychiatrist can give you all the reasons. One theory has to do with the possible failure of a young man's early heterosexual experiences, but—to debunk that theory—many of us grew up with miserable first attempts at sex, and we turned out to be heterosexual. In fact, according to the most recent Kinsey survey, about 20 percent of the gays interviewed had been married at one time and considered their marriages to be "moderately happy."

Many men who grew up in a mother-dominated household (held by some to cause homosexuality) still ended up choosing the straight life. I wonder if we will ever know the complete answer to your question.

*Q. Do homosexuals run into the same problems as other men, such as impotence and premature ejaculation?*

You bet. All men have the same problems. The gay life does not necessarily mean a trouble-free sex life. Far from it. The majority of homosexuals have reported the same hang-ups as we "straights": the inability to get and maintain an erection and coming too fast for their partners. They also have the same problems in trying to get their mates to respond to their sexual requests. "Not tonight, I have a headache" seems to prevail in both gay and straight societies.

*Q. I'm gay, but so far I've stayed away from anal intercourse. I keep hearing about serious injuries to the rectum.*

You've heard right. They can be horrendous, but that holds true for any rectal intervention: kids who are horsing around or adults who are drunk or stoned.

I have personally recovered a great many foreign objects from the rectum. In my intern days at Bellvue Hospital, I'll always remember finding my first Coke bottle up somebody's rectum. Because the bottle had been put in warm and then cooled off, it created a negative suction. I had a devil of a time getting it out until I realized all we had to do was drill a hole in the bottom of the bottle, neutralizing the suction. I have found broom handles, pieces of vacuum cleaner attachments, and other strange things. In the urinary tract, stuck into mens' penises, I've discovered everything from peanuts and olive pits to chewing gum, parafin and polyethylene tubing.

Regarding anal intercourse, if there is poor lubrication you can get a tear in the rectum. You may get fissures or hemorrhoids. When a fist is introduced into the rectum, one of the most serious problems that occurs is rupture of the intestinal wall.

*Q. I am not gay, and I can't believe your last answer. Are you telling me that a fist would fit into a man's rectum?*

Not only a fist, but even part of the forearm. I read about one technique where the insertion took place up to the elbow. This is called *fisting* in the homosexual community. I neither condone it nor condemn it. I am merely reporting it.

The man having this done to him must be relaxed, so he may take something like amyl nitrite (a popper) to loosen his muscles and keep them from getting torn. The inserter irons out the anal opening with one finger, moving it from side to side, then inserts progressively two, three, four fingers—and finally the entire fist. If he has not cut his fingernails, is wearing a ring or a sharp object, or is too vigorous, he may rupture the other man's intestine. If this condition is not taken care of promptly by operative intervention, the man will die.

*Q. I've been gay for years, and I would never think of doing what you just described. I think it's perverted.*

There are extremes in both homosexuality and heterosexuality, and most gays and straights stay clear of these practices that could be labeled S.M. (sado-masochism). But they do exist and are not that uncommon. In the gay world, it might be fisting. In the straight world, there are those who are into whips, chains, discipline and bondage, even suffocation. Both worlds merge when injuries occur and these people end up either in a doctor's office or a hospital emergency room. If physicians try to pretend these acts don't exist, they would never be able to diagnose the situation and treat the patient.

*Q. Hasn't the straight world come a long way in accepting the homosexual over the past few years?*

Hardly, when you consider that in thirty-one states homosexual activity, even between consenting adults, is still considered a criminal offense. Hardly, when you consider that two-thirds of the American people still view homosexuality as obscene and vulgar. Hardly, when most people still label gays in occupational ghettos, such as ballet, interior design, and hair styling. How would you like to be a "straight" in one of those professions today? Hardly, when you are told that you must be living a "sick" life of regret and must fervently hope that some day you will be "cured."

Remember, also, that a vast segment of our population still considers every homosexual to be a child molester: "Here comes a fag. I'd better hide my kid." In point of fact, most child molesters are heterosexual in nature and exhibit psychosexual disturbances.

*Q. Many women never report a rape, because they don't want all the publicity and don't want to be humiliated by the police and the press. What happens if a gay male is raped?*

The same thing holds true for any involuntary sexual relationship. Of the gay community, 60 to 70 percent admit to having been victims of rape themselves, either by another guy or by a group of "super machos" trying to humiliate him. Where can the gay go to complain? The police may laugh at him. If he pursues the case and identifies his tormentors, the fear of reprisal is very strong.

*Q. I'm not gay. Seven years ago, as a young man, I was picked up in a small town for a traffic violation and put in jail for the night. In the cell block, five men raped me and hurt me so badly I had to have stitches inside my rectum. When I was put back into the same cell and found one of the same men approaching me again, I went beserk, and beat him badly. I was prosecuted for that and sent away to the state penitentiary for a year—all because of that traffic violation. I've recovered physically, but emotionally, I don't think I ever will.*

I hope everybody pays attention to this pathetic story. It is occurring much too frequently. I know instances where, if a man was to be returned to jail, he would injure, hang or shoot himself, anything, rather than go back and be humiliated again. Many of these people have had to undergo extreme psychotherapy almost perpetually. It's tragic. Why do we continue to protect the rights of the aggressor and ignore the victim?

Society has destroyed this man's life!

# Contraception

Many of us can relate to the trauma the young teenager went through in the movie "The Summer of '42" when he bought his first condoms. If you remember the scene, he had to make several trips into the drugstore: once because there was a woman shopper there and again because he just couldn't say the word *rubber*. In those days, that unmentionable product was kept discreetly hidden behind the pharmacist's counter, just as products like Kotex and Modess came camouflaged in plain brown wrappers.

What a difference from then to now! As *Time* magazine reported, "Suddenly condoms have become respectable. Produced in dazzling colors, materials, and designs, these most ancient of male birth control devices can now be openly displayed in forty-six states, along with cough syrups and skin creams. Though exact figures are kept secret, sales have climbed to 150 million dollars a year, probably double that of five years ago. Condoms have even become something of a symbol of today's more liberated women, who buy them off the bright new display racks" ("Birth Control—New Look at the Old," January 10, 1977, p. 53). So, we see a rapidly changing sexual society making the full circle. Back to basics.

*Q. Why are people going back to basic devices?*

I'm glad you used the word "people," because women are going back to diaphragms just as rapidly as men are returning to rubbers.

The women have actually led the way. They are alarmed by the potentially dangerous side effects of the "pill." Although there may have been some overreaction, still, once one tampers with the endocrine glands in the body, one is opening the door for potential illnesses, such as cancer, in later life.

There is a general dissatisfaction with I.U.D. devices. The family practitioner is, once again, finding himself in the business of fitting diaphragms and instructing his patients in their use.

When her diaphragm is not available, many of today's young women are asking that their partners use a condom, even if they themselves have to do the purchasing.

Remember that poignant scene in "Saturday Night Fever" where the young girl waited for John Travolta outside the disco, hoping he would make love to her and holding out two condoms?

*Q. If the condom is man's oldest contraceptive device, how far back does it go, and how has it changed through the years?*

It goes back to Italy in the sixteenth century. In those days, the earliest models were made of *linen*, which later gave way to the intestines of sheep. Later, lubricated fish skins were used and, for that matter, still are.

The first vulcanized rubber condom was the hit of the 1876 Philadelphia Centennial. Reports have it that people turned away from the agricultural exhibits to stare at this new phenomenom. Each year, over 700,000,000 rubbers are sold in the United States alone. Perhaps we have all taken part in helping to pay for the Goodyear blimp.

*Q. I've heard there are all kinds of kinky condoms on the market, like "French ticklers." Do devices like these really exist?*

Of course, although they are usually associated more with pornography shops than pharmacies. Some of these contraceptives have bumps or knobs built into the outside of the sheath. Others come with a wide, umbrella-shaped tip to supposedly stimulate the vagina.

Since we know that a woman's orgasmic center is not in the vagina, but in the clitoris, what good are all these baubles, bangles, and beads? However, if masquerades and costume balls turn you on, enjoy.

*Q. Isn't the sex act less satisfying to a man if he has to wear a condom?*

There is some truth to that. Basically, a rubber is an extra layer between the penis and vagina. With regard to feeling, it could be likened to shooting pool with your gloves on. You have partially eliminated the sense of touch between you and your partner. And you are also missing the joyful experience of ejaculating your fluid directly into your mate. This is another reason why diaphragms are so much back in vogue again.

*Q. You mentioned how tough condoms are. Does that mean they are "fail-safe"?*

Yes, they retain the seminal fluid. Statistics from large birth control clinics show that they are better than 90 percent effective. Condoms come in all prices and grades, from prelubricated fish skins to basic rubber. Most are coated with a spermicide. The poorer the quality, the more likely the condom is to break. I'd suggest you stick to a middle-grade condom of one of the better name brands. As with everything else, you get what you pay for.

Before you breathe a complete sigh of relief, let me mention one common situation where it is definitely not a "fail-safe" device. After you lose your erection, if you're not careful, the condom and the penis will separate. Then, of course, the rubber and its contents will end up in your partner's vagina.

*Q. Haven't they been working on a male contraceptive pill?*

Yes. Dr. Alvin Paulson, at the University of Washington, has shown that a pill for men is no longer a dream. A daily dose of a new drug, called danazol, has cut the production of sperm in about 85 percent of his test subjects. These were all vigorous young men, who were rendered infertile for the period of this treatment.

I'm not at all sure that better things in life come to us through chemistry. As in the female "pill," we still don't know what the long-term side effects are. There have been reports of decreased sex drive with this drug. Other medications that have been found to lessen sperm counts include nitrofurantoin (a urinary antibiotic), stilbesterol (a female hormone), and testosterone (the male hormone). Recent family planning groups returning from China note that there is a cottonseed derivative, which blocks sperm production, being used for male contraception there. American laboratory tests have indicated that large doses of this substance have proved fatal in animals. The final word is not yet available on this particular preparation. Swedish research now indicates that a *nasal spray* may affect the body hormones, thereby suppressing sperm production. If this proves true, you could clear out your nose and testes at the same time.

*Q. Didn't you say that in the event one or both partners has herpes, a condom becomes the only acceptable device?*

Yes. The condom ranks as the Number One device to prevent the transmission or retransmission of sexually transmitted diseases. Another of its medical uses is to break up a highly contagious disease such as trichomonas, commonly known as Trich disease. This ping-pong germ is exchanged back and forth very easily by sexual contact. The only way to stop this "game" is to put both partners on medication and to employ a condom. Thus there is no interchange of vaginal secretion into the male urethra, or urethral discharge into the vagina.

*Q. It is my understanding that there is a Buddhist sect in India who have developed a system of birth control by teaching themselves to ejaculate inwardly?*

I've read about that, but I'm not terribly familiar with it. Here's what would happen: there are two valves at the neck of the bladder. The weaker of the two is above the prostate gland, and the stronger, below, at the start of the urinary passageway. Ejaculation occurs between these valves. It is possible to train yourself to relax the inner valve while tightening the outer, and, thereby not ejaculate in the normal manner. This is a common occurrence after a man has had a prostate gland operation where the inner valve has been removed or widened. He also may then find himself ejaculating backwards.

I imagine men could be taught to do this with considerable practice.

*Q. Then couldn't this method become the ultimate in birth control?*

No. The ultimate answer is orange juice. You don't take it before or after. You take it *instead!*

Seriously, prior to ejaculation, lubrication of the urinary passageway and of the seminal canal takes place from glands lining this area. And when that occurs, some sperm can inadvertently leak out, prior to full ejaculation. Backwards or forwards, inwards or outwards, sperm means babies.

*Q. I read where if you keep your scrotal area very warm, that can act as a means of contraception?*

Temperature control of the scrotal area is advised for problems of infertility, not contraception.

For example, sometimes we have men who cannot cause impregnation take *cold* showers or baths about an hour before intercourse. The theory is chilling the scrotum increases the chances of getting vigorous sperm. For this type of infertility problem, we also advise loose fitting clothing: boxer shorts instead of jockey shorts and non-crotch-crunching trousers.

So, getting back to the original question, yes, by *increasing* the heat in the scrotum, you *decrease* the chance of sperm production.

Notice that I said "the *chance.*" Maybe you would want to gamble on a hot bath as a contraceptive device. I wouldn't.

*Q. We've heard about "coitus interruptus," especially among teenagers, where the boy promises he will pull out before he ejaculates. Does this work?*

No. I'd prefer to see him doing his gambling in Las Vegas. Sperm are present in the lubricating fluid that emerges from the penis during sexual excitation, even before actual ejaculation occurs. And as far as his "promise" goes, what does he tell the girl later? "I lied?"

*Q. What about the rhythm method?*

You know what you call people who use rhythm? PARENTS.

The critical period of ovulation varies too much from month to month to make this method reliable. There are, on the market, a number of devices, ranging in price from $15 to $300, that supposedly pinpoint the exact time of ovulation. The problem here is there are too many variables, such as time of day, emotional stress, food intake, and fatigue. And these devices must be used for several months before any specific pattern emerges. Interestingly enough, although they were originally designed for the purposes of fertility, they are now being used to designate the "safe" period.

*Q. What is the most unusual type of birth control you have seen?*

One in which your friends and neighbors decide *for* you (1) *if* you should have any children at all and (2) if so, how many.

On a recent trip to mainland China, I learned that in order for a family to reproduce, they must first get permission from their commune. There is a general meeting to decide if it is in the interest of the commune to have additional babies. Most often, the family will be allowed one child—two at the most.

But you have to remember that sex is not a big thing to the Chinese. They usually marry in their thirties, and up to that point, they have never been exposed to sexuality in the media, as Western cultures know it. I saw men walking hand in hand with other men, and women holding hands with other women for companionship, not because of homosexuality. But I didn't see many young couples on the streets.

With later marriages and small families, it is obvious that the Chinese are getting birth control information. From what I learned, once a couple has had their "quota" of children, it would not be surprising if the commune decided that the husband should undergo a vasectomy. So, in a way, the Chinese communal system represents the ultimate in birth control.

# Vasectomy

Most of us are becoming increasingly aware of the consequences of unrestricted population growth, particularly as it relates to the future of our children. A child born today will have to live in a world that has five times as many human beings on it as are alive right now. Fortunately, man is beginning to realize that contraception is a two-way street and not simply a woman's problem. Current cultural attitude changes include the growing recognition of women's rights and a lowering of religious and legal barriers to contraception.

Responsible couples now question the wisdom of continuing to bear the cost, the inconvenience, and the failure risks of conventional methods of birth control.

They won't trust the rubber again. They have tried the diaphragm with contraceptive jelly and find it a messy, troublesome procedure that robs the sex act of spontaneous pleasure. The rhythm method is far too risky. The "pill" has many side effects; and the I.U.D., often poorly tolerated, has a high risk factor. Voluntary male sterilization, called vasectomy, has now become the most popular American contraceptive.

Vasectomy is certain and simple, a "sexual emancipator," for it permanently frees a man from fear of causing impregnation. It is a simple and most dependable procedure. Yet vasectomy, both legally and ethically, is clouded with fear and misinformation. Male sterilization erroneously has become equated with castration; as virility has historically been equated with the ability to reproduce.

Let's try to clear up a few things before getting into the questions and answers.

The first function of the male testicles, or testes, is to manufacture microscopic sperm cells. The sperm travel from the *scrotal sac,* located between a man's legs, through two hollow, soft, spaghettilike *tubes* called the *vas deferens.* These tubes end in the prostate gland, located within the pelvis. At the time of ejaculation, the sperm mix with fluid from the prostate gland and pass through the penis. During intercourse, when these sperm cells fertilize the female egg, the result is conception.

*Q. How do you do a vasectomy?*

The word *vasectomy* comes from the Greek word *vas*, "vessel that brings down," and *ektome*, "to cut." One or two small cuts are made in the scrotum to expose the cords (vas), from which a small section is removed. Then the severed ends are seared, to block them, and are sometimes tied. Finally, the scrotal edges are brought together, and a supportive dressing is applied. No vital organ or blood vessel is touched during this procedure.

*Q. How strongly do you feel about precounseling for a patient who is considering a vasectomy?*

I insist on it. I spend *at least* one hour counseling each prospective patient. I use an anatomical sketch pad to show him exactly what the procedure is designed to do. I give him a fact sheet to read and a booklet called "What About Vasectomy?" put out by the California State Department of Health, Office of Family Planning (1978). I encourage him to discuss all his questions and doubts with me.

I examine the patient and show him exactly where the surgical cuts will be made, where his vas is, and how to prepare himself. I will advise him to have a jock strap ready to use afterward, to support his testicles. Crushed ice in a plastic bag should be applied to the scrotum after surgery to prevent pain and swelling. I also counsel his female companion, explaining her role after surgery.

I strongly believe in extensive precounseling. Some of my colleagues prefer to show a video tape explanation to the patient. That just isn't my game plan. Since this is a highly personal decision that the patient must make, I feel that the give and take of a one-to-one personal discussion is far more satisfactory.

Two articles I suggest that the patient read are "Who's Afraid of Vasectomy," by Marvin Grossworth (*Saturday Review*, June 10, 1972), and "Birth Control for Men," by Elizabeth Connell (*Redbook Magazine*, July 1972).

*Q. Do I have to go into a hospital for a vasectomy?*

Not usually. This is primarily an office procedure done under local anesthesia. I use an intravenous medication, such as Valium, to tranquilize the patient and relax his muscles. When he is relaxed, he isn't pulling up his testes, so I do not have to fight to pull them down during the surgery.

The whole operation takes about an hour—from the time he comes into the office, until he leaves. The actual cutting time is probably about twenty-five minutes.

The patient should remain quiet for a day after surgery. However, if he has a desk job, there is no reason why he couldn't return to work on the second day. Those involved in heavy, physical jobs may require several additional days' sick leave.

Complications such as swelling, bleeding, or infection may occur, but are rare.

*Q. Are there any complications from the medical standpoint?*

Yes. For example, the man who continues to have sperm in his ejaculate after the vasectomy. If there is one thing a urologist doesn't need, it is to have the "next of kin" named after him.

Some call this complication the "myth of the *third* cord." And that's what it is—a myth. There IS no third cord. What probably has happened is that the same cord (vas) has been tied or cut twice, and the other cord never touched.

Another possible complication could involve bleeding into the scrotal sac, a soft tissue area without a bone to stabilize it and thereby limit the swelling. I've seen swelling as large as a grapefruit occur if the patient resumes vigorous physical activity too soon.

Infection may occur in the incision, but it is usually mild and can be cleared up by local warm soaks.

But these complications are the exceptions, not the norm.

*Q. I had a vasectomy recently, and it wasn't quite as easy as you said. I got a lump that gave me a lot of discomfort.*

That is possible. If some spermatic fluid leaks out, right where the cut is made, you can get a painful little lump. It's called a *foreign body reaction* or a *granuloma*. However, with our modern techniques we've noticed a great decrease of this complication.

*Q. What happens to the sperm?*

Vasectomy will not allow the sperm to leave the body. Although the sperm continue to be manufactured, they have nowhere to go. They are just reabsorbed by the body.

*Q. When am I safe? When can my wife and I forget about pills, diaphragms, the whole schmear?*

Leftover sperm will remain in the vas above the cut end through approximately twelve ejaculations. So contraception must continue until two semen checks show a total absence of sperm. After that, I advise a yearly checkup.

Essentially, the same amount of fluid will be ejaculated from the prostate gland after vasectomy as before. However, this fluid will be sperm free. The man, in effect, will be shooting blanks. Fewer than 1 in 10,000 vasectomies "don't take," or fail.

*Q. What about psychological or emotional problems following a vasectomy?*

First, we try to "head this off at the pass" with some good, solid precounseling in the office. Vasectomy in men who have strong religious beliefs against contraception may result in disabling guilt complexes.

Age also has a lot to do with it. A young man in his twenties, who is heavily into zero population growth, may change his mind in later years. A man who feels he already has his family must realize that he may lose his children through an accident or his wife through divorce or death. He may remarry and want children by his next wife.

Married couples most often consider vasectomy because it is easier for him to be sterilized than for her to have her tubes tied. Sometimes he has been pressured by his mate into having the procedure done, when he really doesn't want to. A number of patients, either during precounseling, or on the actual day of surgery, simply walk out of the office. If they are this reluctant, I think that they are right. To do a vasectomy on these men would be entirely wrong.

A vasectomy will never save an unhappy marriage. That's why I prefer to meet with both husband *and* wife.

Some women tend to question the masculinity of the man undergoing vasectomy, as some men question the femininity of women after hysterectomy. Probably, these individuals found that the danger of pregnancy added spice to their love lives. Now, it's gone. How immature!

The vasectomy patient should be a well-oriented man who understands the procedure, wants the procedure, and has a supportive partner.

*Q. What does a vasectomy cost?*

You can figure on an average of $250. This would include counselling, surgery, post-operative care and semen analyses.

*Q. Does medical insurance cover it?*

Even though a vasectomy is an elective operation (like cosmetic surgery, it doesn't *have* to be done), yes, it is covered by most medical policies.

*Q. How do I really know if a vasectomy is for me?*

First and foremost, this must be your decision. A vasectomy should never be done to please someone else or to "keep up with the Joneses." Think it over carefully. Be sure you want *no* children. There are so many uncertainties in life that it is impossible to predict *now* what you may want in the future.

*Q. Can I "hedge my bet" and freeze some sperm ahead of my vasectomy?*

There has been a lot of publicity about sperm banks—and I wish I could say good publicity. One man had his frozen sperm in a bank near San Francisco when the current went off, thawing his "deposit." Many of the sperm banks have proved financial failures and the specimens were consequently destroyed. But the major problem is with immobility. The longer you keep sperm frozen, the less mobile they are when thawed. And it takes mobile sperm to fertilize. Ideally, sperm should be frozen no longer than from six to twelve months, which places it time wise, very close to the surgery. Occasionally, an infertile man with too few or too weak sperm may try to save his own semen in frozen portions. Later this is thawed, pooled and used as a single artificial insemination. The active sperm rate of such a procedure is virtually zero. Frozen semen simply has not done very well except in animal husbandry.

*Q. What about sex after a vasectomy?*

Enjoy! It may be even better now that you have peace of mind. Remember, while the first function of the male testes is to manufacture sperm, the second function of the testes is to produce the male hormones responsible for the masculine physical characteristics and the sex drive. These hormones are distributed throughout the body and are totally unaffected by a vasectomy.

Your sexual drive and your ability to perform will *not* be diminished. The operation will not have the slightest effect on your sexual desires. Your hair will still grow. And you voice will *not*, repeat, *not* suddenly change from basso profundo to quivering tenor.

You will have freed your life, and your mate's life as well, from mechanical devices and chemicals. Relax and savor your victory.

*Q. My husband had a vasectomy about four years ago, and now he seems to have colds all the time. Is there any correlation?*

No, there isn't. At many universities and family planning centers, vasectomy patients have been followed for many years, just to see what might develop.

At first we thought there might be a higher incidence of gout, since as the sperm break down, uric acid is released and picked up in the system. This hasn't proved true.

There was also a question of whether there would be a higher incidence of prostate gland enlargement. Again, negative. Incidence of cancer and respiratory infections have been checked in hundreds of thousands of men who have had vasectomies. There has been no correlation between the procedure and subsequent disease.

People tend to blame any and all later symptoms on vasectomy: premature aging, multiple sclerosis, even liver failure. Some women report increased menstrual flow and cramping after their partners' sterilization. While it may be convenient to blame life's disappointments on the surgery itself, there is absolutely no relationship.

*Q. Wait a minute. I just read about a possible connection between having a vasectomy and arteriosclerosis.*

If I were an aging ape, I'd be concerned about it, since the report originated from a primate research center. One group of elderly and not particularly healthy apes underwent vasectomy. A control group did not have the operation. But all the apes were fed a high-fat diet. Some time later it was found, on examination of their blood vessels, that the vasectomy group had a larger degree of arteriosclerosis.

So far, there have been no reports connecting this condition to vasectomized men.

*Q. I had a vasectomy years ago. Unfortunately, I also had a divorce. My new bride-to-be wants children. Can a vasectomy be undone?*

Absolutely. And if the sterilization was done within the past ten years, the success rate is 90 percent.

It has been made possible by a new technique, pioneered in Australia, using microsurgery to reconstruct the severed vas. With 64-power magnification we are able to blow up the visual field in such a way that we can take suture material (as fine as hair), and sew the cut vas back together end to end, like two pieces of wet spaghetti.

But I'll make no bones about it—this is major surgery, involving many hours under the microscope.

Please remember that a vasectomy reconstruction, although successful in its own right, does not necessarily restore your fertility.

*Q. By re-hooking the spaghetti, does that mean everything will work again?*

Not necessarily. There are many factors involved. First, before actually performing this operation, your doctor will take a smear from the lower portion of the vas (that portion near the testicle) and make a slide right in the operating room to make sure you have sperm. In other words, the surgeon deliberately tries to "milk" sperm out of the vas to be certain you are producing them. If there are two good solid ends that can be put together, your chances of success are 90 percent, as far as sperm passage is concerned, from the testes up the vas.

*Q. For the 90 percent of the vasectomy reversals that are successful, are there any other problems that can crop up?*

Yes, infertility may continue, despite a successful reversal. At the time of the original surgery, if sperm tended to leak out into the tissues, the man might be effectively *vaccinating himself* against his own sperm, forming antibodies. So even if healthy sperm are produced, after vasectomy reversal, they may be worthless as far as fertility is concerned.

The only possible solution for this condition is use of an antibody suppressing medication such as cortisone. Even this treatment is very "iffy" and works in less than 50 percent of the cases.

Remember, *time* can be your friend or your enemy in any vasectomy reversal. If you wait over ten years, the chances for success aren't very good. If you are already in the eight-year range, and if you are considering it, you'd better get cracking.

*Q. This sounds considerably more expensive than the vasectomy itself.*

You'd better believe it! Costs on this reconstruction can range from $1500 to $3000. That's why we stress so much counseling prior to the vasectomy. So, again, be sure you want that vasectomy in the first place. The tragedy is that so many young people in their twenties are demanding vasectomies. They're often back again before they are thirty, asking to have the vas rejoined, probably having changed wives several times in the interval.

Make sure your marriage is stable and that you really don't want more kids. I strongly urge anyone in his twenties not to even consider a vasectomy. Too much life is still ahead of him. We now even find teenagers asking for this operation. I simply won't do it, and neither will most of my colleagues.

*Q. I wish I had the problem of whether or not to have a vasectomy. I was born without any vas deferens, and I'd like to have children. Can anything be done for me?*

This condition is unusual, but it does exist. You produce sperm, but there is no communication between your testes and the ejaculatory duct. So the sperm can't come out.

Since you still ejaculate fluid from your prostate gland, one possibility would be to pool your semen with that of a donor. That could, indeed, result in your becoming a father—at least, in name, because it could be either your or the donor's semen that actually did the trick.

# Fertility

After two sections on how *not* to have children, it is only fair to give the loyal opposition its due. I'm talking about those couples who *want* to have children but can't. This seems to involve a growing number of people today, who feel unfulfilled if they don't have a family. It is incredible how many folks are coming into my office with a desire to have children. I find this particularly gratifying.

Up to *20 percent* of all marriages are *barren*. We can help almost 80 percent of this group, if they just seek medical advice. For the other 20 percent, we can't do a darn thing because we don't know what factors are responsible. There could be depression, psychological problems or inherent congenital defects that we simply don't know that much about. We may be able to diagnose them, but we can't cure them. No one really knows the silent, painful suffering of the childless couple who are subject to the questions and pressures of well-meaning families and friends. Their motivation to continue the family line is strong.

In our culture, male fertility and virility are considered one and the same, even though they have nothing to do with each other. But, if the problems are mainly psychological, the longer a couple waits to seek help the worse the situation can become. Devastating effects can build up, leading to decreased libido, lessening achievement of orgasm, and temporary impotence. A once-relaxed sex life becomes stressful and complicated. Romance is lost as partners find fault with each other. A sense of depression and unworthiness pervades. That's why it is so important to talk about it, to air it out, and to see if medical science can help.

The *man* is the *main factor* in *30 percent* of all barren marriages today and a *contributing* factor in another *20 percent*. Infertility in the male leads us into many possible areas. There may have been a past illness that contributed to his present inability to produce sperm. He may never have developed the adequate tissue from which to develop sperm. He may have a thyroid, adrenal, or pituitary hormone deficiency or excess. Maybe one or both of his testicles descended late, and he lost the capacity to produce sperm. There are a number of factors to be measured in a fertility check, such as hormonal levels and sperm counts. It isn't just the *number* of sperm, as we used to think, but the *quality* of the sperm that counts (Amelar, Dubin, and Walsh, 1977).

If the sperm cannot actively swim upstream, like a salmon spawning, then they cannot cause fertilization. Once ejaculation has occurred within the vagina, the sperm are pulled up into the uterus (or swim into the uterus) and then up into the tube, where the egg is fertilized. You can have a beautiful sperm *count* (over 60 million sperm for every 30 drops of semen), but if they don't move they don't fertilize.

Let me describe this transportation system from the beginning, to illustrate how a problem might occur along the way.

Sperm are manufactured in the testes, and it takes many weeks before they even leave that area. Then they start to transport themselves into the epididymis, the little cap gland that sits above the testicles, where they mature. Later, they migrate slowly up the vas into a reservoir behind the prostate gland, where they rest until the moment of ejaculation. But, from the time of production until ejaculation occurs, a period of almost *ninety days* elapses from the very first appearance of the initial cell until it is ejaculated.

*Q. In the infertile male, do these cells simply not appear in the first place?*

They may appear, but they may be immature, or they may be over the hill as far as their ability to fertilize. Old sperm just won't cause fertilization. There is no such thing as poor sperm causing poor fertilization. That doesn't exist. You either get good sperm and fertilization that "takes," or you don't. The question is not the quantity of the sperm as much as their ability to be transported.

*Q. If the sperm are not being transported, wouldn't it then be possible to take a sample of the sperm from within the testes and then, by artificial insemination, fertilize the woman?*

It's been tried, but it doesn't work, and here's why. As the sperm move up from the testes to the reservoir behind the prostate, they are encased in a gelatinous substance and are inactive.

At ejaculation, sperm are activated by enzymes in the secretions of the prostate gland. When a man ejaculates, about 99 percent of his seminal fluid comes from the prostate. That fluid contains the enzymes and the sugar (or fructose) that activate the sperm and dissolve the gelatinous capsule around them. It also boosts them a bit, helping them to move.

Sperm drawn directly out of the testicle itself lack these enzymes and sugars. Such sperm are immobile at this stage and cannot fertilize.

*Q. My wife and I don't seem to be able to have children. I've noticed a soft swelling around my left testicle. Could this be the cause?*

If you look at yourself in the mirror, you'll notice that your left testicle usually hangs lower than your right. The reason for this is that the blood vessels supplying the left testicle are longer than the ones supplying the right. Because of this extra vessel length, sagging occurs, so around the left testicle there is a puddling of blood that looks like a bag of worms. It is really a collection of varicose veins, or, varicocele. It is not uncommon and sounds like what you've got.

A varicocele has been found responsible for decreasing both the number and motion of sperm. To correct this condition, your doctor ties off these varicose veins. An incision is made, not in the scrotum, but in the abdomen. Using a local anesthetic, your surgeon picks up the dilated vein, ties it off, and cures the variococele. And bingo! In about 50 to 60 percent of such cases, not only does the sperm count improve but also the mobility of the sperm is increased.

*Q. Is this an office procedure?*

Not really. I prefer this to be done in a hospital, even though the patient may be in and out the same day.

*Q. Is it possible for a man to be unable to father children in one marriage, yet be successful in another, even though both wives were proven to be fertile?*

The answer is *yes*. A man may be just as fertile in both marriages, but his fertility index may vary with different partners. One mate may form antibodies against his sperm, which cause them to lose their effectiveness, whereas the other mate does not. A man with a low count and poor sperm motility may have little success with Woman A, yet the vaginal chemistry and autoimmune blood factors in Woman B may actually enhance his sperm capability to effect fertilization. Tests are available to check these factors.

*Q. As a man grows older, are his sperm just as fertile?*

Absolutely. If you've got sperm and if they are moving, age has absolutely nothing to do with it. Look at Charlie Chaplin, Senator Strom Thurmond, and Bing Crosby, who started whole new families in their later years. Age is not a factor. Transportation and maturation are.

*Q. What can you tell by the sperm's appearance?*

Normal sperm have oval heads that are tapered at one end. The tail emerges from the rounded side. These are the "good guys"—able to fertilize.

The other sperm cannot. They may be too young or too old. Two-headed, large-headed, or small-headed sperm, or heads without tails—all fall into this category.

*Q. I think that has been my husband's problem, the abnormal-looking sperm. Is the situation hopeless, or can something be done about it?*

It depends on the cause. First, we would check his hormonal balance. Then, we'd look for an inflammation or disease of the testes. If the trouble is here, we can treat it.

Once we rule out those possibilities, a biopsy of the testes should be performed, not for possible cancer, but to evaluate their functional capacity to produce sperm. If that ability is lost, we can do nothing more about the situation.

*Q. If there is a hormonal imbalance, how can that be treated?*

First, we would check the hormones of the pituitary gland, which govern sperm and male hormone stimulation, growth factors, and prolactin. Prolactin is a hormone which when present in above normal amounts produces milk in the female but can suppress sperm production in the male.

If we find any abnormalities in these pituitary hormones, we advocate use of pituitarylike injections known as HCG *(human chorionic gonadotropin)*. This is the same medication that is employed in many weight-reduction programs. The idea here is to stimulate the testes to produce more sperm and male hormone. This is not a one-shot injection but may involve long periods of treatment, depending on the results of the sperm analyses.

*Q. Are there any side effects—like, will the man grow massive hair all over his body?*

If he does not shave daily or if he is deficient in pubic hair as a result of the hormonal imbalance, the answer to your question is yes. He may grow more hair, but in the usual places, not all over his body. We're not going to create an orangutan.

*Q. I read a newspaper article about a new drug called bromocriptine. How is it being used?*

Some men produce too much prolactin from their pituitary gland, and the excess not only suppresses fertile sperm production but depresses sex drive as well. Bromocryptine, a new substance first produced in Europe, neutralizes these effects. Although only available abroad originally, this medication has recently been approved by the Food and Drug Administration (FDA) for American usage.

*Q. Before a man starts to consider injections and surgery, aren't there some more practical things to try first?*

Of course. What we are striving for is fertilization. Most women know when they are ovulating, because they get a little pain in the middle of their monthly cycle. There may also be a day when they show a little blood on a napkin, and they know that ovulation occurs at that time.

That egg can be fertilized over a period of seventy-two hours. The couple should plan intercourse approximately forty-eight hours prior to the time ovulation occurs, have it daily, and continue it forty-eight hours after that time. Remember, the egg has a seventy-two-hour span. Under ideal conditions, the sperm will live about forty-eight to seventy-two hours inside the woman. So what we are doing is bracketing the time period when egg and sperm can get together.

Also, for generations, alterations in body temperature, on a monthly basis, have been used by women to predict the time of ovulation. This has been proven unreliable.

There is a third approach called the "fern test" which involves your doctor's taking a vaginal smear on a daily basis to pinpoint the exact time of ovulation.

The important thing to consider is that sperm are produced by the body. The healthier the body, the better the sperm. Here is where nutrition enters the picture. Protein is the basic building block of the body, so I emphasize a protein diet rich in *liver*. (I realize many of you are saying "yecchh," but it works.)

*Q. Does sexual position play a part if you're trying to conceive?*

Yes. The "missionary" or "male superior" position is the best. That way, ejaculation will occur in a position where the semen will run uphill toward the woman's cervix. Incidentally, the man should stay *in* as long as he can afterwards. That way, his penis will act like a plug, aiding the vagina to retain the semen.

I also suggest that the woman's hips be propped up on pillows, so that her legs are up but the middle of her body is down. She could even put her feet up on a wall.

The other thing I suggest, which we mentioned in the section on contraception, is for the man to take a cold shower before sex. The lower the body temperature, the better chance for good sperm. And he should turn in his tight-fitting pants and briefs for looser apparel.

*Q. Now that medical science has made the great breakthrough in creating the first test tube baby, might this be the answer to all fertility problems?*

No. Just consider, in the United States alone, there are over *three million couples* who are barren. This is an extremely involved procedure that necessitates repeated surgery to obtain and then reimplant the fertilized egg. We really don't know what the failure rate is going to be until we have more case histories to study.

Before you pack your bags and head for a research center, there are other options to be considered. The sperm is the smallest cell in the male body and is extremely susceptible to such outside influences as job-related chemical exposure, radiation exposure, or stress.

For the infertile male, the same drug that has been used to create ovulation in women who don't ovulate, clomiphene, has been found to goose up the sperm's activity. Arginine, an amino acid, has also been found to restore fertilization capability to sperm in some cases.

There is also research into the effects of caffeine on suppressing or improving the motility of sperm. Coffee, mixed with ejaculate, seems to make the sperm move faster. Whether it was regular grind or instant has not been established.

*Q. Having babies isn't our problem. But, after three daughters, we would really like to have a son. Is there some way to increase our odds on this?*

I'm sure you know by now that the father alone determines the sex of the baby. His sperm are labeled *male* and *female*. Now, I don't mean there is a Macy's sticker on each one, but the male-coded sperm are more active and shorter lived. So, if you want a boy, sex should take place *just* before ovulation.

I might jokingly suggest that the mother-to-be stay off bumpy roads and give up jogging for a while to reduce the possibility of the genitals being shaken off her scion.

If you have the reverse problem and are tired of raising a basketball team, intercourse should occur thirty-six to forty-eight hours before the calculated time for ovulation. This way, we have eliminated the majority of male sperm in favor of the longer-lived, slower, female-coded sperm.

There has been a theory that calls for a baking soda douche, if the couple desire a boy, just before intercourse. If a baby girl is preferred, a douche with white vinegar is the ticket. However, I feel this has not been substantiated. These aforementioned ingredients are probably far more effective in your kitchen than in your bedroom!

*Q. With all the publicity of Planned Parenthood and Zero Population Growth, why all the sudden interest in fertility? Isn't the world already overpopulated?*

Many couples still feel the need to raise a child—the one-for-one replacement theory. Years ago, the infertile couple would go to a private or government adoption agency and take their pick of unwanted babies. In most cases, the exact attributes of the parents could be matched: color of eyes and hair, intellectual capacity, and so on.

Today, because of liberalized abortion laws, the pill, and the tendency of single women to keep their babies, the adoption pool has dried up. Couples who are determined to find a blond, blue-eyed baby are having to turn to the "Gray Market," making under-the-counter payments of up to $25,000 in many instances. These adoptive parents also open themselves to the possibility of having the natural parent threaten to or actually claim the child at some unfortunate future time. No wonder a couple will go to any extreme to solve their own problems of infertility.

*Q. You keep emphasizing the need for sperm to move in order to cause fertilization. At what speed do sperm travel?*

We estimate that the sperm travel about the rate of half an inch in four minutes. At the time of ejaculation the sperm take about eight minutes to enter the uterus and the tubes so that this is the time we estimate from the time of ejaculation to the time of first conception.

# Drugs and Aphrodisiacs:
# Uppers and Downers and Nothingers

We are, literally, inundated these days with "street drugs": everything from weed and superweed to cocaine, LSD, Quaaludes, amphetamines, hashish, and heroin. For those who have turned to any of these concoctions purely to enhance their sexual prowess, they might as well try chicken soup.

I'm serious. A physician in Pittsburgh became acutely ill with pneumonia. After three days of taking chicken soup, he improved. When the doctor took him off chicken soup, he promptly got sick again.

Then they tried antibiotics, which didn't work. So they put him back on chicken soup. He got better and finally left the hospital.

Dr. Laurence Green, Professor of Urology at the Mayo Clinic, humorously noted that there was a special ingredient in chicken soup. In fact, he gave it a four-line technical name, which he summarized as being "Schmaltz." Then, with tongue in cheek, he added, "Schmaltz, as manufactured by Upjohn."

He declared this magic compound could eliminate impotence. When applied in ointment form to the penis, it could increase the libido and prevent premature ejaculation, and was definitely dose-related. If a 5 percent ointment was used, you could have intercourse for five minutes, a 15 percent ointment would give you fifteen minutes, and so on.

Then he tried to get some volunteers to see if this was a valid study or not, and they planned to do a double-blind test, but no one would participate unless assured that he would be in the group that got the Schmaltz!!

If a man thinks that chicken soup can make him a better and longer-lasting lover, fine. At least, he's not going to do himself any harm. With street drugs, you're talking about a whole new ball game. Just break down the phrase: *drugs*—for every medication, there are side effects; and *street*—*that's* where you buy them and *that's* why you have no idea just what you are getting.

And what *are* these so-called love drugs you can buy on the street?

Arthur Stickgold (1978), chairman of the Los Angeles County Drug Abuse Task Force, listed them for *Playboy* Magazine:

1. *Butyl Nitrite.* Available as a "room deodorant" in head shops. "It is easy to take prior to an orgasm, allowing you to get suddenly stoned just before coming. . . . It is generally safe unless it leads to a blown blood vessel, in which case it can kill you."
2. *Quaaludes* or *Ludes.* "If you are a strongly inhibited person, Ludes will greatly enhance your sex life. If you are uninhibited, the depressant effect of the drug will make you perform like a log."
3. *MDA.* An amphetamine-based drug similar to mescaline. Some users report "it increases *sensuality* rather than sexual performance." Others experience joyless erections. Amphetamine-based drugs "hop-you-up" by suppressing fatigue. They also alter perception.

With the widespread use of drugs available today, I wonder if people are not more interested in changing their perception of themselves as lovers more than in learning how to actually become better lovers. At best, only transitory improvement in sexual activity can be gained with the use of drugs. At worst, you can kill yourself. How do these people handle themselves when the drugs run out and they must confront one another in stark sobriety? Do they just skip sex until they can afford to make a buy and change their self-images again?

Transitory improvement is just that—transitory! It will not break old patterns or build a better self-image on a permanent basis. If you are having sexual problems, there is better help available than street drugs.

*Q. I seem to function at my best when I'm stoned. How do you feel about marijuana?*

I wish I knew. I find myself changing my mind with every new conflicting medical report. I suppose pot does heighten the awareness of the sex act, makes it more colorful and intense. You say you function better? Fine. But aren't you basing this belief on the clouded memory of your personal experiences while in the drug state? I'd be much more interested in discussing how you feel while in a period of unaltered perception.

We do know that marijuana does not improve sexual performance at all. As a matter of fact, there is considerable literature out that suggests it decreases performance, by lowering male sex hormone levels, due to its influences on the pituitary gland. All men produce both male and female hormones. If you reduce one or the other, the ratio changes, and the female hormones become more dominant.

With habitual users definite feminizing may take place, leading to an enlargement of the male breasts. Furthermore, a marked decrease in sperm count and sperm motility has been reported, along with an increase in the number of abnormal sperm. To add to my confusion, as well as everyone else's confusion, another group reports that there is no hormonal change at all. It's beyond me. You'll have to make up your own mind.

*Q. Could pot smoking affect whether you can get pregnant or not?*

You bet. I just discussed the changes in the male sperm count and motility. In the female, one shot of THC, the injectable form of marijuana, equal to one street joint, will lower levels of the two basic ovarian hormones which influence fertility.

Even though pot may reduce the chances in both male and female of becoming daddy and mommy, don't count on it as a method of birth control.

*Q. Why is everyone suddenly talking about cocaine? Why has it become so "in"?*

Like marijuana, coke started as a ghetto drug and most people paid very little attention to it until recently. Now it's become the big "show biz" turn on because it stimulates erotic desire and fantasy.

And it's not just the drug that's the turn on. It's all the paraphernalia that goes with it: the gold-plated razor blades, the silver spoons, and so on. There are a lot of folk that are walking around with tiny spoons hanging from their necks that have never taken a snort in their lives.

Like amphetamines, cocaine gets you "up" fast. You are super alert and your feelings are intensified. You are usually among a group of close friends and the whole thing becomes a ritual. The host says, in effect, "You are my trusted few."

What happens if you take too much coke, too soon? After the initial hit, your pulse and breath slow down; and you may experience convulsions or stomach pain. With long-term usage, coke can lead to paranoia and hallucination.

Current estimates show that there are some sixteen million people using marijuana in the United States. Only about 10 percent of this number, or roughly, 1,600,000 are reputedly into cocaine. And I doubt if that number will increase much, due to the current street price, which can range up to $150 per gram.

In *Paris One*, novelist Matthew Brady would have us believe that cocaine, rubbed on the penis, can delay ejaculation and heighten the woman's sexual awareness as the drug comes into contact with her clitoris.

Evidently, Mr. Brady has had more experience than I have had along this line. My experience is zilch! I have my doubts.

*Q. I keep hearing about "poppers." What are they?*

Sort of a poor man's cocaine. Poppers are actually isobutyl nitrite or amyl nitrite. Their effects are similar to cocaine. Since they have been classified as nonprescription drugs, a lot of manufacturers have rushed them to the marketplace under such trade names as "Bullet," "Locker Room," and "Rush." Many of the pornographic bookstores carry one form or another of poppers. A recent estimate came up with the figure of 5 million Americans who are inhaling these chemical ampules fairly regularly.

When you "sniff a popper," time becomes distorted and you feel that you have a supererection and a prolonged orgasm. But poppers can lower your blood pressure and dilate your blood vessels, and, in patients with heart disease, can possibly cause a coronary artery blowout. Some of the side effects are nausea, headaches, and possible damage to liver and lungs.

*Q. What about alcohol? Does it stimulate sex or depress it?*

It can do both. Shakespeare was correct when he wrote that alcohol provoked desire but diminished ability. In small amounts, alcohol can increase the interest in sex but decrease the actual performance, due to failure of blood flow to the penis.

There have been many recent studies on acute alcoholism with college students who "tied one on" over a weekend. By Sunday night, researchers found that their blood testosterone, or male hormone level, was practically zero. So a lot of booze in a short period of time can really do you in.

Our major concern in the chronic alcoholic is liver disease, or cirrhosis, which leads to increased fat deposits and scarring in the liver. The liver is your body's prime detoxifier. By cleaning out body poisons, it takes what is left and makes it usable. When cirrhosis occurs, there is a change in the normal sex hormone ratio. The male hormones are altered, so the female hormones become more dominant. When that happens, you can say "bye bye" to your sex live—or your wife may have already kissed you off because of your drinking.

*Q. I read an article in Reader's Digest called "Is Your Sex Life Going Up in Smoke?" Is there any correlation between smoking and diminished sexual prowess?*

Yes. The problem with smoking has been well documented for years. We know that if you take an isolated piece of tissue from the human stomach for research purposes, and then blow smoke onto it, you can see the blood vessels absolutely constrict down. The smoke causes a chronic reaction, around the blood vessels, which creates scarring. These vessels simply do not dilate as well as before.

That's why we think that smoking and ulcers are highly related. Smoking can also cause the same type of blood vessel changes in the penis, which affects the male's sexuality. And need we say more about the dangers of bladder and lung cancer?

Every cigarette package says: "Warning: The Surgeon General Has Determined that Cigarette Smoking Is Dangerous to Your Health." I'll go one step further: It can directly lead to your death. And death can really play hell with your sex life!

*Q. What other kinds of things are considered as "uppers" these days?*

Have you heard about Levo-Dopa, or L-Dopa? Used primarily in treating Parkinson's disease, this preparation affects certain areas of the brain so that an erection comes, but the desire doesn't. In fact, people into L-Dopa seem to have numerous erections, but they can occur at any time and are completely unpredictable. This, of course, can prove quite embarrassing. Hallucinatory psychotic episodes are part of this picture.

The National Heart Institute is researching a drug called PCPA. While experimenting with this drug on patients with heart conditions, they found that these people were becoming almost uncontrollable, sexually. PCPA is not yet available on the market, with or without a heart condition.

From the European front come KH-3 and bromocriptine. KH-3 is nothing more than Rumanian Novocaine which is given intramuscularly or orally. I visited Dr. Anna Aslan, the original researcher, in Rumania several years ago and from what I could tell, all her ninety-year-old patients who had been taking this medication looked ninety and functioned like ninety. I saw no apparent change. Here in the United States, university studies indicate that the main effect of this drug is probably as an antidepressant.

Bromocriptine, as reported in *Chemical and Engineering News*, alters an abnormal excessive secretion from the pituitary gland which decreases sex drive. As of now, this product has just become available in the United States.

If you buy *any* of these on the street, look out!

*Q. You are talking about "uppers and downers." What do downers have to do with sexuality?*

Destroy it. No one who wanted to increase his sex drive would even *think* of taking a downer.

But he might be taking downers right now and not even know it. *Your worst enemy may be your own medicine chest!* The most commonly prescribed drug *in the world* today is *Valium*. This, along with other tranquilizers, can decrease your awareness to the point that you can't even *think* about sex, or about anything else for that matter. Although inhibitions may be eased by Valium, tranquil means tranquil.

Antihypertension drugs can interfere with your nerve endings. They will bring your blood pressure down, and your penis along with it. Those of you taking drugs for ulcer or bowel problems have deliberately impaired your muscular activity and your penis's, as well. Pain killers—even aspirin—may interfere with the function of the prostate and prevent erections. Probably the only safe thing in your medicine cabinet is your toothpaste. And even that has sugar in it.

*Q. For years, I have heard about something called "Spanish Fly." Does it exist? What is it, and does it turn a woman on?*

Oh, it exists all right. It's the most famous historical aphrodisiac in human conversation. And that's where it belongs—in human conversation. The only practical sexual use of Spanish Fly is on the farm, where it is used for pig mating, since it makes the sow more receptive to being mounted. The correct medical term is Cantharides. It was originally made from ground beetles, although it has now been synthesized.

I would hardly call it a turn on for either sex, since it can cause tremendous blistering and irritation of all the mucous membranes in both the male and female. It can hit the eyes, the rectum, the nose, the urethra—every mucous membrane. It is that powerful. In fact, physicians often use it to burn warts off patients. So, if you have warts and your doctor suggests using this stuff, don't think he is "on the make."

*Q. Every drugstore seems to have a big display of musk preparations. Is this supposed to be a big turn on?*

Don't ask me. Ask a small, female Asiatic deer, since musk is gathered from the secretion beneath the foreskin of the male buck. It is now used as a fortifier in many perfumes, and it supposedly makes the fragrance last longer.

I can think of one practical usage. If you lost your mate in the woods, she might be able to track you down more quickly.

*Q. Right next to the condom display in my drugstore, I've seen a rack of tubes called "Control." I am told that, if I rub this on my penis, it will make sex last longer.*

There has been a rush to the marketplace of a whole series of these promissory preparations: "Control," "Delay," "Detain," "Maintain." They are all pretty much the same and contain a mild local anesthetic in a cream or ointment base. They claim to reduce the sensitivity of the head of the penis by dulling the feeling.

In some men, it may be slightly effective. In most cases, not at all. At least, it can make you feel great while it is being rubbed on.

*Q. What about the ancient standby—ginseng?*

You were right to use the adjective "ancient." The use of ginseng dates back over 5,000 years. Ginseng is supposed to have great mystical powers to increase a man's prowess and retain his virility. I think the best thing going for it is that the root *looks* something like a man.

Like all other herbal teas, it is refreshing, even if it doesn't do anything for you sexually. And stick to the tea, which is healthier for you than ginseng in cream or capsule form.

*Q. There is a mystical store near me that advertises "love potions" like bats' blood. I don't think they are dangerous, like street drugs, but might they do me any good?*

Yes and no. Yes, most of them are not dangerous; and, no, they will not turn you into a superstud.

Aphrodisiacs to supposedly heighten sexual drive date back to ancient Egypt, about 2,000 B.C. And they include (are you ready for this?) pine nuts, bats' blood mixed with donkey's milk, dried salamander, menstrual fluid, tulip bulbs, the fat of camel's hump, salted crocodile, pollen of date palm, the powdered tooth of a corpse, wings of bees, ground crickets, the genitals of hedgehogs, the blood of executed criminals, swallows' hearts, vineyard snails, and powdered stag's horns. Need I go on? Need I say more?

Still, the best aphrodisiac is your own imagination.

*Q. What do you think about vitamin E?*

It has been of some value in treating leg cramps. Also, it has been proven that brown rats don't get gray hair while taking large doses of it. Now, it may not seem terribly important to you whether or not a rat's sideburns turn white; but there is active research going on now into the relationship between vitamin E and the slowing down of the aging process.

What are the actual facts? I wish I had more of them. Perhaps vitamin E helps conserve oxygen, vital to your body cells. Look, vitamin E may help. But, as with any other food substance that you are not used to, start slowly with low doses. Work up to 1,600 units a day, over a long period of time. Just make sure you get the pure alpha tocopherol type which is less irritating to the stomach than the mixed tocopherols that come in a linseed oil base. You can also get vitamin E in its natural state —in unrefined vegetable oils, unroasted seeds and nuts, and raw wheat germ.

*Q. What can stimulate the average man?*

Anything. And I mean *anything:* a pretty girl, a flower, a perfume, a song, a pro football huddle. You name it. But, never being completely content, man has always searched for that extra something that will put him an additional step up on his sexual ladder. It was once believed that powdered lions' penises and rhinoceros' *horns* had aphrodisiac qualities. (Now you know where the term "horny" originated.) Even today, you can buy these products at street-corner herbalist shops in the Far East, along with tigers' balls, hippo snouts, and pieces of whale.

*Q. Why is my doctor reluctant to give male hormones, when I have read that they will improve my sexual activity?*

We can measure testosterone (male hormone) levels in the blood. Most men are not deficient, so this whole procedure is usually valueless and has potential dangers. In middle aged or older men, there is a greater tendency towards cancer of the prostate. While this is a latent condition, it can be activated by indiscriminate use of male hormones for rejuvenation purposes. If you insist on receiving these hormones, frequent physical examinations are a must.

*Q. Let's get specific. Are oysters important?*

Only to one another.

# In Conclusion

So MANY HAVE said to me about sex, "All people do is *talk, talk, talk* about it; *read, read, read* about it; *watch, watch, watch* it." I feel it is far, far better to be occupied with sex than preoccupied with it. That is my reason for writing this book.

I have attempted to explain the lifestyle of the male body. The rest is up to you. This is not a how-to book. We have enough of those already on the market.

In the summer of 1978, two of the nation's top ten books explained, in great detail, *how* to run or jog. Now I ask you—if you were suddenly being chased across a pasture by a crazed bull, would you turn to your *how-to* book to find out *how* to put more distance between you and the approaching pointed horns?

Syndicated columnist Art Hoppe (1977) summed it up beautifully. Art created a mythical guru, Maharishi Luke Drebbing, who was looking for the secret of a successful sex life. After reading every possible report, survey, exposé, and how-to book on the subject, the Maharishi eventually came to this conclusion: "The cause of everyone's sexual hang-ups is *reading* all these books and articles dissecting everyone's sexual hang-ups. Indeed, my research has proven conclusively that anyone who reads another word about sex will be *totally unable* to engage in that activity *ever again.*" Who can refute such wisdom?

Communicate with your mate and express your feelings openly. The one thought I have hoped to convey is "Learn to relax and just let life and love happen."

And if I might be allowed to open six Chinese fortune cookies, these are the final thoughts that would crumble out:

1. Sex is good for your health.
2. Eat right.
3. Exercise.
4. Try different techniques.
5. Love-making is not a competitive sport.
6. Use it or lose it.

# References

Allen, T. D. "Microphallus." *Journal of Urology* 119 (June, 1978): 750-753.

Amelar, R.D., Dubin, L. and Walsh, P. C. *Male Infertility*. Philadelphia: Saunders, 1977.

Arehart-Treichel, J. "Teen Pregnancy—A New Epidemic," *Science News* 133 (May, 1978): 229, 302.

Bailey, H. *GH3*. New York: Bantam Books, 1977.

Beck, L. F. *Human Growth*. New York: Harcourt Brace Jovanovich, 1969.

Bell, A. and Weinberg, M. *Homosexualities: A Study of Diversity Among Men and Women*. New York: Simon & Schuster, 1978.

"Birth Control—New Look at the Old." *Time* 109 (January 10, 1977): 53.

Bitschai, J. and Brodny, M. L. *History of Urology in Egypt*. Private printing, 1956.

Blount, J. H., Darrow, W. W., and Johnson, R. E. "Venereal Disease in Adolescents." *Pediatric Clinics of North America* 20, no. 4 (November, 1973): 1021-1034.

Bogert, L. J., Riggs, G. M. and Calloway, D. H. *Nutrition and Physical Fitness*. Philadelphia: Saunders, 1966.

Boyd, M. *Take Off the Masks*. New York: Doubleday, 1978, pp. 2, 161.

Brody, J. "Sterilization." *New York Times*, 4 April 1971, Section IV, p. 7.

Brody, J. E. "If You're Thinking of Getting a Vasectomy," *San Francisco Chronicle*, 28 November 1978, p. 28.

Butler, R. V. and Lewis, M. I. *Sex After Sixty*. New York: Harper & Row, 1976.

California State Department of Health, Office of Family Planning. *What About Vasectomy?* Booklet B. 1978.

Cant, G. *Male Trouble*. New York: Praeger, 1976.

Caplan, H. W. and Black, R. "Unrealistic Sexual Expectations." *Medical Aspects of Human Sexuality* 8, no. 8 (August, 1974): pp. 8-36.

Caroline, N. L., and Schwartz, H. "Chicken Soup. Rebound and Relapse of Pneumonia: Report of a Case." *Chest* 67 no. 2 (February, 1975): pp. 215-216.

Chang, T. W. "Genital Herpes." *Journal of the American Medical Association* 238, no. 2 (July, 1977): 155.

Child Study Press. *What to Tell Your Child About Sex.* New York: Child Study Association of America, 1974.

Cilento, R., and Felshman, N. *Sex Forever.* Chicago: Playboy Press, 1977.

Cockett, A. and Urry, R. *Male Infertility.* New York: Grune and Stratton, 1977.

Colton, H. "The Real Sexual World of Teen-agers." *Forum* 7 (September, 1978): 18-23.

Comfort, A. *A Good Age.* New York: Crown, 1976.

———. *Joy of Sex.* New York: Crown, 1972.

Committee on Medical Education. *Assessment of Sexual Function.* Vol. 8. New York: Group for the Advancement Of Psychiatry, 1973.

*Complications of Vasectomy.* Fact Sheets M-1, 2, 3. New York: Association For Voluntary Sterilization.

Connell, E. B. "Birth Control For Men." *Redbook* 139, no. 3 (July, 1972): 10-12, 13.

Crespo, J. H., and Rytel, N. W. "Venereal Disease." *American Family Practitioner* 18, no. 2 (February, 1978): 90-101.

Debrovner, C. and Shubin-Stein, R. "Sexual Problems Associated with Infertility." *Medical Aspects of Human Sexuality* 10 (March, 1976): 161-162.

Dermange, H. "Aphrodisiacs." *Sexual Medicine Today* 2, no. 10 (October, 1978): 25-26.

Diagram Group. *Man's Body.* New York: Paddington Press, 1976.

Donegan, F. "Loveable Feasts." *Viva* 5 (February, 1978): 20, 70, 109, 111, 113.

Dubin, L. and Amelar, R. D. "Varicocele." *Urologic Clinics of North America* 5 (1978): 573-583.

Dunbar, R. E. "For Men Only: Foolproof Birth Control." *Look* 35 (March 9, 1971): 45-46.

Dunbar, R. E. and Bush, I. M. *A Man's Sexual Health.* Chicago: Budlong Press, 1976.

Ehrlich, G. E. "Restoring the Arthritic's First Loss—Sexual Rehabilitation." *Sexual Medicine Today* 2, no. 9 (September, 1978): pp. 6-10.

Faigel, H. C. "A Developmental Approach to Adolescents." *Pediatric Clinics of North America* 21, no. 2 (May, 1974): 353-360.

Feltman, J. "Antioxidants, Aging and Cancer." *Prevention* 30 (July, 1978): 62-67.

Fenwick, R. D. *The Advocate's Guide to Gay Health.* New York: Dutton, 1978.

Finkle, A. L. "Psychosexual Problems of Aging Males: Urologist's Viewpoint." *Urology* 13, no. 1 (January, 1979): 39-44.

Frank, E., Anderson, C. and Rubenstein, D. "Frequency of Sexual Dysfunction in Normal Couples." *New England Journal of Medicine* 299, no. 3 (July 20, 1978): 111-115.

Freedman, H. "Infertility." *Forum* 8, no. 4 (January, 1979): 45, 47-50.

Gaskell, P. "The Importance of Penile Blood Pressure in Cases of Impotence." *Canadian Medical Association Journal* 105, (February, 1971): 1047-1051.

Gittelson, N. "What Should We Tell the Children." *McCalls* 10 (January, 1979): 153-156.

*Gonococcal Infections*. Stanford University Medical Center Memorandum, January 31, 1977.

Goodman, B., Rosenbaum, M. and Bardach, V. H. "Sexuality and the Physically Disabled." *Bulletin New York Academy of Medicine* 54, no. 5 (May, 1978): 499-564.

Goodman, L. S. and Gilman, A. *The Pharmacological Basics of Therapeutics* . (5th ed.). New York: Macmillan, 1975.

Gordan, G. G., Altman, L., Southren, A. L., Rubin, E. and Lieber, C. S. "Effects of Alcohol Administration on Sex Hormone Metabolism in Normal Men." *New England Journal of Medicine* 295, no. 15 (October 7, 1976): 793-797.

Gottlieb, B. "Sex and Nutrition: A Perfect Marriage." *Prevention* 30, no. 4 (April, 1978): 73-77.

Graham, E. "Vasectomies." *Wall Stret Journal*, 11 November 1970, p. 1.

Green, Richard, ed. *Human Sexuality, A Health Practitioner's Text*. Baltimore: Williams and Wilkins, 1975.

Greene, L. F. "Letters to the Editor." *Chest* 68 (1975): 605

Grosswirth, M. *The Truth About Vasectomy*. Englewood Cliffs, New Jersey: Prentice-Hall, 1973.

Hallberg, E. C. *The Gray Itch*. Los Angeles: Ombudsman Press, 1977.

Havemann, E. "Re: Senior Sexual Fears." *Cosmopolitan* 184 (June, 1978); 241-244.

*Herbal Aphrodisiacs*. San Francisco: Stone Kingdom Syndicate, 1971.

Hill, J. "Penile Study." *Forum* 7 (September, 1978): 62-65.

Hobson, D. and Holmes, K. K. (ed's.). *Nongonococcal Urethritis and Related Infections*. Washington, D. C.: American Society for Microbiology, 1977.

"The Homosexual Clinic." *Sexual Medicine Today* November 3, 1976, pp. 42-43.

Hoppe, A. "Sex Made Easy." *San Francisco Chronicle*, 17 January 1977, p. 37.

*Human Sexuality*. Chicago: American Medical Association, 1972.

Hunt, M. *Sexual Behavior in the 1970's*. Chicago: Playboy Press, 1974

Jones, H. B. "On the Problems Executives Must Anticipate with the Growth of Marijuana Smoking." *Executive Health* 14, no. 1 (October, 1977).

Kaplan, H. S. *The New Sex Therapy.* New York: Quadrangle/The New York Times Book Co., 1974.

Katchadourian, H. A. and Lunde, D. T. *Fundamentals of Human Sexuality.* (2nd ed.). New York: Holt, Rinehart, and Winston, 1975.

Kaufman, R. F. *Better Sex, Better Marriage.* New York: Morrow, 1978.

Kinsey, A. C., Pomeroy, W. and Martin, C. *Sexual Behavior in the Human Male.* Philadelphia: Saunders, 1948

Klugo, R. C., and Cerney, J. C. "Response of Micropenis to Topical Testosterone." *Journal of Urology* 119 (May, 1978): 667-668.

Kounovsky, N. *Shape-Up for Super Sex.* New York: Delacorte Press, 1977.

Lang, G. and Sackler, A. M. "The Love Lore of Lust Provoking Foods." *Sexual Medicine Today* 2 (December, 1978): 16-18, 33.

Leboyer, F. *Birth Without Violence.* New York: Knopf, 1975.

Leif, H. I. (ed.). *Medical Aspects of Human Sexuality.* Baltimore: Williams & Wilkens, 1975.

Lerrigo, M. O. and Cassidy, M. A. *A Doctor Talks to Nine- to Twelve-Year-Olds.* Chicago: Budlong Press, 1969.

Levinsohn, F. and Kelly, G. L. *What Teen-Agers Want to Know.* Chicago: Budlong Press, 1967.

Lewis, S. "How Diet Can Help Your Love Life." *Ebony* 31, no. 8 (June, 1976): 84-86, 88-90.

Lipshultz, L. (ed.). "Male Infertility." *Urologic Clinics of North America* 5, no. 3 (October, 1978): 433-436.

Lobsenz, N. "Sex and the Aged." *New York Times.* 15 January 1974, p. 13.

Love, J. "A Consumers' Guide to Condoms." *Forum* 8, no. 4 (January, 1979): 75-80.

Mann, P. "The Truth About Safe Marijuana." *San Francisco Chronicle*, 7 August 1978, p. 14.

Marshall, J. J. "Some Hard Looks at Male Sexuality." *Human Behavior* 7 (September, 1978): 62-65.

Masters, W. H. and Johnson, V. E., *Human Sexual Inadequacy.* Boston: Little, Brown, 1970.

———. *Human Sexual Response.* Boston: Little, Brown, 1966.

Mayle, P. *What's Happening to Me?* Secaucus, N. J.: Lyle Stuart Press, 1975.

———. *Where Did I Come From?* Secaucus, N. J.: Lyle Stuart Press, 1976.
McBride, W. and Hardt, H. F. *Show Me*. New York: St. Martin's Press, 1975.
McCabe, C. "Age of Advice." *San Francisco Chronicle*, 11 September 1978, p. 39.
McCarthy, B. *What You Still Don't Know About Male Sexuality*. New York; T. Y. Crowell, 1977.
Menning, B. *Infertility*. Englewood Cliffs, N. J. : Prentice-Hall, 1977.
Morrison, J. M. B. "The Origins of the Practices of Circumcision and Subincision Among the Australian Aborigines." *Medical Journal of Australia* 1 (January 21, 1967): 125-126.
Moskowitz, R. D. "Gay Doctors Group First in the U.S." *San Francisco Chronicle*, 25 July 1978, p. 20.
Murphy, S. J. *The History of Urology*. Springfield, Ill.: Thomas, 1972.
Murray, L. "New Hope for the Spinal Injured-Sexual Rehabilitation." *Sexual Medicine Today* 2 (January, 1978): 4-9.

National Institute on Drug Abuse. *Marijuana and Health*. Rockville, Md., 1976.
Nelson, B. J. "Managing the Boy with Undescended Testes." *Sexual Medicine Today* 2 (October, 1978): 20-32, 33-35.
"The New Morality." *Time* 110 (July 3, 1978): 5-8, 111-115.
"NGU: The Cinderella Drug." *Time* 112 (July 17, 1978): 73.

Orloff, E. "Herpes." *San Francisco Examiner*, 30 September 1978, p. 12.

Paige, K. "The Ritual of Circumcision." *Human Nature* 1, no. 5 (May, 1978): 40-48.
Palmquist, A. and Stone, J. *The Minnesota Connection*. Warner Books, 1978.
Passwater, R. *Supernutrition for Healthy Hearts*. New York: Dial Press, 1977, pp. 94-96.
"Penicillin Resistant Gonorrhea." *Health Bulletin; San Mateo. County Department of Public Health* 41, no. 1, 1977.
"Physician's Exposure to Nudity." *Sexual Medicine Today* 20 (August 20, 1975): 13-15, 20-21.
Pietropinto, A. and Simenauer, J. *Beyond the Male Myth*. New York: Quadrangle/The New York Times Book Company, 1977.
Preston, E. N. "Whither the Foreskin?" *Journal of the American Medical Association* 213 (September 14, 1970): 1853-1858.
Prilook, M. E. "Dos and Don'ts with Herpes Genitalis." *Patient Care* 12, no. 3 (February, 1978) pp. 121-151.

Quinn, P. S. "Why So Many Men Lose Interest in Sex." *Cosmopolitan* 185 (September, 1978), pp. 218, 227-229.

Ratcliff, J. D. "I Am Joe's Bladder." *Reader's Digest* 104 (February, 1974): 73-76.
———. "I Am Joe's Gland." *Reader's Digest* 97 (November, 1970): 92-95.
———. "I Am Joe's Pituitary Gland." *Reader's Digest* 101 (November, 1972): 158-161.
———. "I Am Joe's Prostate." *Reader's Digest* 99 (December, 1971): 99-102.
Reckless, J. and Geiger, M. "Impotence as a Practical Problem." *Disease-A-Month*, May, 1975.
Remondino, P. C. *History of Circumcision from Earliest Times to Present.* Philadelphia: Davis, 1891.
Rueben, D. R. *Everything You Always Wanted to Know About Sex But Were Afraid to Ask.* New York: David McKay, 1969.
Robertson, W. H. "Teenage Pregnancies." *American Fertility Society Newsletter* 11, no. 5 (August, 1977): 2.
Rotkin, I. D. "Herpes Simplex Type 2." *Journal of the American Medical Association* 235, no. 20 (May 17, 1976): 2188, 2189.
"Rushing to a New High." *Time* 112 (July 17, 1978): 16.

Sadock, B. Kaplan, H. and Friedman, A. *The Sexual Experience.* Baltimore: Williams and Wilkins, 1976.
Saltman, J. *Marijuana: Current Perspectives.* New York: Public Affairs Committee, 1976.
Sandholzer, T. A. "S.T.D.'s—Paradox of the Sexual Revolution Impact." *AMA News*, October 27, 1978, pp. 1, 2, 12.
Sattler, F. D. and Ruskin, J. "Therapy of Gonorrhea." *Journal of the American Medical Association* 240, no. 21 (November 17, 1978): 2267-2270.
*San Mateo County Department of Public Health and Welfare Annual Public Health Clinic Report.* 1977.
*Santa Clara County Department of Public Health and Welfare, Annual Venereal Disease Report.* 1978.
Satterfield, S. "Common Sexual Problems of Children and Adolescents." *Pediatric Clinics of North America* 22, no. 3 (August, 1975): 643-652.
Schultz, M. G. "Giardiasis." *Journal of the American Medical Association* 233, no. 13 (September 29, 1975): 1383.
Schultz, P. "When Your Plumbing Rusts." *Esquire* 89 (April 25, 1978): 32-33.
Sciarra, J. J., Markland, C. and Speidel, J. *Control of Male Infertility.* New York: Harper & Row, 1975.

Seligman, J. "Notes on the Significance of Circumcision." *Journal of Analytic Psychology* 10 (1965): 5-21.

Shapiro, H. I. *The Birth Control Book*. New York: St. Martin's Press, 1977.

Shanor, K. *The Shanor Study*. New York: Dial Press, 1978.

Sheehy, G. *Passages*. New York: Dutton, 1976, pp. 304-320.

Shepard, M. "Ecstacy." *Moneysworth Manual* (1977).

Silber, S. J. "Vasectomy and It's Microsurgical Reversal." *Urologic Clinics of North America* 5, no. 3 (October, 1978): 573-584.

Sloan, D. and Africano, L. "Masturbation: A New Look." *Forum* 7 (September, 1978): 29-32.

Soffer, A. "Chicken Soup of Laetrile. Which Would You Prescribe?" *Archives of Internal Medicine* 137 (August, 1977): 994-995.

Spock, B. "What I Think About Nudity in the Home." *Redbook* 45, no. 3 (July, 1975): 29, 31, 33.

Starr, R. "Surgery for the Sexually Misbegotten." *Harper's* 256 (May, 1978): 48-56.

"Sterilization. The New American Contraceptive." *Sexual Medicine Today* 2 (October, 1978): 6-11, 40-43.

Stickgold, A. "Streetwise," *Playboy* 25 (September, 1978): 167, 225.

Stein, R. "The Sexually Assertive Female." *San Francisco Chronicle*, 11 January 1977, p. 13.

Strong, B., Wilson, S., Clark, L. D., and Johns, T. *Human Sexuality: Essentials*. St. Paul: West, 1978.

Tavris, C. "Good News About Sex." *New York* 9 (December, 1976): 51-57.

———. "Men and Women Report Their Views on Masculinity." *Psychology Today* 10 (January, 1977): 35-42, 82.

Tobe, J. *Your Prostate*. Ontario: Provoker Press, 1967.

"Undoing Sterilization." *Newsweek* XCII (February 28, 1978): 77.

Walsh, P. C., Wilson, D., Allen, T. D. et al., "Clinical and Endocrinological Evaluation of Patients with Congenital Microphallus." *Journal of Urology* 120, no. 1 (July, 1978): 90-95.

Waugh, M. "A Sexually Transmitted Disease: Enterobius Vermicularis," *Medical Aspects of Human Sexuality* 4 (September, 1976): 119-120

Weiss, C. "Motives for Male Circumcision Among Preliterate and Literate Peoples." *Journal for Sex Research* 2, no.. 2 (July, 1966): 69-88.

Wershub, L. *Urology from Antiquity to 20th Century*. St. Louis: Green, 1970.

"What's It Like to Be a Man?" *San Francisco Examiner*, 1 April 1976, p. 21.

Wood, R. Y. and Rose, K. "Penile Implants for Impotence." *American Journal of Nursing* 78 (February, 1978): 234-238.

Wylie, E. M. "Birth Control for Men." *Reader's Digest* 98 (January 1971): 53-58.

Zilbergeld, B. *Male Sexuality.* New York: Little, Browm, 1978.
Zucchino, D. "Sex Revolution—All Talk, No Action." *San Francisco Examiner*, 13 January 1979. p. 10.

# Index

Crabs, 90–91
Cranberry juice, effect on urine, 54
Cremaster muscles, 36
Crosby, Bing, 135
Cystoscope, 27, 57
  examinations with, 48–49
Cysts, sebaceous, 31

Danazol, 122
Development, stages of (male)
  adolescence, 3–4
  anal, 2
  genital, 2
  latency, 3, 71
  oedipal, 2
  oral, 1–2
  phallic, 2
  pre-puberty, 3
  puberty, 3
Diabetes
  as cause of impotence, 97
  effect on urination, 53, 55
Diaphragms, 120, 121
Dimethyl sulfoxide, to increase penis
  size, 26
DMSO. See Dimethyl sulfoxide
Doctor, difficulty of finding if
  homosexual, 112–113, 114
Dorsal slit, 13–14
Downers, effect on sexuality, 145
Dreams, sexual, 67
Drugs, effects on sexuality, 140–148
  alcohol, 143–144
  amphetamines, 141
  anesthetics, 146
  antihypertension drugs, 145
  aspirin, 145
  Bromocryptine, 145
  butyl nitrite, 141
  cocaine, 142–143
  downers, 145
  ginseng, 146–147
  KH-3, 145
  L-Dopa, 144
  "love potions," 147
  marijuana, 141–142
  MDA, 141
  musk, 146
  oysters, 148
  pain killers, 145
  PCPA, 144
  "poppers," 143

Quaaludes, 141
  smoking, 144
  Spanish Fly, 145–146
  testosterone supplements, 148
  Valium, 145
  vitamin E, 147
Dry cleaning, related to bladder cancer,
  57
Duke's Test, 122
Dysentery, among homosexuals, 115

Eggs, benefits of eating, 77
Egyptians, ancient, circumcision among,
  10
Ejaculation
  amount of, 45
  effects of prostate surgery on, 44, 123
  inability to have, 95
  inward, 44, 122–123
  "limited number in life" theory, 73,
    111
  and penetration, time between, 60
  premature. See Premature ejaculation
Elderly. See Senior citizens
"Empty nest" syndrome, 63
Endemic, defined, 83
Enlarged prostate. See Prostate, enlarged
Epidemic, defined, 83
Epididymus, 134
Erection
  change with aging, 106
  crooked, cause and cure, 27–28
  devices to aid in attaining, 28–30
  morning, 50–51
  saltpeter, effect on, 27
  too many, 26–27
Erythromycin, 87
Estrogen supplements, to treat female
  menopause, 107–108
  side effects, 108
Eunuchs, 39
Exercise, effect on sex life, 74–76

Fantasies, sexual, 67, 70
"Fern test," 137
Fertility, problems with, 132–139
  causes, 133–134, 135, 136
  Duke's Test, 122
  effect of marijuana on, 142
  numbers of barren, 133, 138
  positions best for conception, 137–138